Arie Itamar

Misty Mists

to

Derek

with love and friendship

Ariel

2.10.2018

Arie Itamar

Misty Mists

Senior Editors & Producers: Contento De Semrik

Translated from the Hebrew by Tanya Rosenblit

Edited by Sherrill Layton

Designed by Ivan Bogod

Copyrights © 2013 by Contento De Semrik
and Arie Itamar

- ISBN: 978-1533419941

International sole distributor:
Contento De Semrik
22 Isserles, 67014 Tel-Aviv, Israel
semrik10@gmail.com
www.semrik.com

Arie Itamar

Misty Mists

THE EXPERIENCES OF A SIX-YEAR-OLD

On the Escape Route from Europe
to the Voyage on *The Exodus*

Contento De Semrik

This book is dedicated to my children: Orna, Sharon and Avishai, and to my grandchildren: Yonatan, Noa, Adar, Ayala and Noga.

ACKNOWLEDGMENTS

I hereby thank Ada Benishu for her drawings from inside the deportation ship and the photographs from the French press, which she has passed on to me, from the bequest of her late father Ing. Simon Lutzky from Paris.

Special thanks goes to the production team at Contento De Semrik.

Table of Contents

Prologue

A milestone stands on the broken road: "Twenty-one kilometers to Ismaïlia." On the right is the Suez Canal, a strip of water shining in the moonlight on that night in October 1973. On the left are stubble fields, marshes and tall palm trees. The enemy is east of the canal and west of the palm trees and we are in the middle, with a big moon above us. There is a tense silence now after a day of crossing the canal and moving, with smoke, fire, bombings and explosions, and death being so nearby—it sounds like the whistle of a bullet or the whisper of mortar shrapnel. A weird silence, while I stand amidst this quiet. Far in the distance, in the sanatorium among the Sharon Orchards, lies dying the man who has been my father for the last twenty-eight years—my second dad, and I am thirty-three already. Can it be?

Was my age not falsified? Am I not older? And who was my first dad? And why was I an outstanding pupil until the sixth grade but later failed?

I know that the secret lies out there in the distance; maybe in the port city by the Black Sea, maybe in the battlefields of the spacious Russian steppe or in the woods and swamps near the road to Smolensk. My stepfather's dying illuminates these images and events like this moon, and they interlace with each other: Today's bomb noises and the heavy bombarding of the crossing bridge with the German bombings of the train station in Odessa—the port city in 1941. A primitive pump is ticking in the distance and it sounds like a slow squeaking train that moves through the fields and villages of the tired Russian steppe. And I head out to find my past—inside the mists, sailing through the desert road from Rephidim to the Suez Canal—in the days of this war, and then sailing back to the spaces of that faraway, beautiful and cruel land—in the days of that other war. And I swore, for the sake of life here, and for the memory of those that remained there: If I will leave this war alive, I will embark on the long road and tell the story.

And the road is hard and winding, hard and misty, but it is accompanied by songs and melodies: Songs of celebration and melancholic melodies, songs of death and reviving music. And the dead and the living accompany me and march with me into the distant and near past, to days of fear and hope, to sights that I will never forget.

Chapter One

"Artillerymen! You Have Your Orders!"

"With the fire of our love for the motherland burning in our hearts,
We go to mortal battle for the honor of the mother country.
The cities are ablaze, enveloped in smoke.
We move to the forest and the guns.

Artillerymen! You have your orders!
Artillerymen, the homeland calls for us!
From our thousands of guns,
For the tears of our mothers,
For the motherland—Fire! Fire!"

The Artillerymen March
Lyrics: T. Chernikov, music: V. Gusev
Translation from Russian: unknown

Through the song's simplistic words and naïve melody, I see my first father, marching to battle in that big war from which he did not return.

I was a small boy, almost a baby. From the mists of my childhood I remember a small house in the port city of Odessa. My mom and dad were sitting by the window singing songs; but no more. My dad was recruited to the army and days of anxiety and nervousness ensued. My mom kept herself busy with different chores, when suddenly my dad appeared—on vacation, wearing a military uniform with a belt tied diagonally on his shirt with two yellow pencils in his pocket. And I was standing in my crib crying. I didn't know that soldier. Mom would pet me and say: "Why, this is Daddy!" and I cried. The soldier took a pencil from his pocket and handed it to me, but I kept on crying and wouldn't calm down. Later, he was gone, and that's how I saw my father for the last time.

Distant sounds of war were beginning to reach us. We were living with Grandma—a short and fat woman with white hair and a swarthy face. When the bombing sounds approached us, I was carried while we all ran to some place inside the basement of the big house. On the way, I saw a railroad and I knew that we were living near the railway. How can I remember all these things? How old was I? And maybe it is all nothing but fiction.

August 1984. *The small Ilyushin airplane flew for two hours from Moscow to Simferopol—the capital of the Crimea Peninsula on the shores of the Black Sea. The participants of the geological tour are getting sleepy; the local instructors are tense in anticipation for the landing. Beneath me I see vast fields and orchards, and on the horizon is a range of mountains. The airplane has landed and the routine of the small and remote airport unfolded in front of me. We took a bus from the airport to a gray city without grace. The next day we hit the road again, this time to the Black Sea. Along the way, the local instructors stuffed our heads with boring information. But nothing interested me; I wanted to see my birth crib, the Black Sea, the beach. We passed a mountain range with an ancient fortress called "the Jewish Fortress" in Tatar; the bus stopped and a magical landscape was revealed to me. Below was the Black Sea—which got its name due to the black rubble that covers its bottom; the water itself is deep blue. Wooded mountains slide steeply to the beach; this view reminds me somewhat of Haifa. I tried to feel, to sense, whether this landscape is close to me. Does it have something that can steer my memory? But it is difficult for me and I cannot feel anything but the pleasure that the beauty around me provokes.*

We are on the road again, only now we are actually heading to the beach. I am excited; will I finally be able to see that beach—the beach of my childhood—up close? We pass through a series of underground mazes with a number of levels and descend in an elevator that opens into a narrow and long tunnel at the end of which there is light. There, a heavy disillusionment awaits; the "beach" is nothing but endless concrete planes with wooden bunks lying on top with unbearable closeness to one another; a flood of human beings walks by these wooden bunks. Above us are two additional levels of concrete and fences. "Where is the sea?!" I shout with despair at the Russian guide, "where is the beach?!" The guide shrugs his shoulders and answers: "It is what it is. I don't like this view either; there is a real beach but it is far away from here." We went to Yalta; a historic city, a famous palace on the mountainside, another resort. Military-like canisters were standing on the street, out of which the national drink, kvass, is poured for the vacationers. A troublesome rain is dripping down. I approached the pier in the port and saw a ship; its name is Kolkhida, its home port—Odessa. Something moved inside me despite everything. The ancient Odysseus traveled here with his sailors and founded my birth city that is named after him; the legendary Argonauts with Jason traveled here in their ship to the Colchis land en route to the Golden Fleece. An accordion melody is sounded from afar and I listen and my memories are awakened once again.

The frequency and force of the bombings grew stronger. My mom stopped running to the basement and we all stayed with her. She no longer had the strength left to run to and fro. "If we live—we live, and if we die—we die," so she said. The German army was approaching Odessa and the city was almost entirely surrounded. Squads of local accomplices joined the Germans and conducted raids in the area. Rumors about Jewish pogroms were whispered around. Mom was suddenly drafted into the army and it was decided that Grandma would take me and we would both board the first train east, before it was too late, and Mom would join us after she was discharged from the army. Covered in a blanket, half asleep, with sweet lullabies sounding in my ear, I found myself in Grandma's arms on a passenger train on a dark night. Above me was a big window, inside of which tree tops and roofs passed by rapidly.

The train drove on a perilous track that was about to be interrupted by the enemy army. Suddenly bullets penetrated the windows with crashing sounds. Outside, in between the gunfire, wild neighing could be heard. A German cavalry, or local accomplices, savagely attacked the train. Grandma hovered over me with her entire body and told me, "You will live, I don't mind dying," and thus protected me with her big body. Yet before she could do that, a bullet or glass shard scratched my forehead. I don't remember if I cried or if Grandma silenced me; I don't remember if the wound bled or for how long. I was in a daze, my senses were a blur, the train accelerated rapidly, the gunfire passed and I was left with a scar on my forehead.

My memory has awakened in a new city and a new

country—Stalinabad, the capital of the republic of Tajikistan, an eastern Muslim country by the Afghan border. My mother appeared from nowhere and the three of us lived together in a small room adjacent to the movie theatre. The room was, in fact, the theatre's box office and refugees like us resided in the big hall and other rooms in the building. The refugees were mostly Jews and almost all were women and children. The city itself was not big and in its center was a wide long street whose end seemed to merge with the faraway mountains with the snowy tops—the Pamir Mountains.

I started going to kindergarten with kids from different nationalities, Nationality seemed to be very important among the kids. I was teased for being a Jew—"Jyd" they called me—and I would come home torn up inside and hurt. I was also teased for my last name and children would call out "wolf, wolf" (my name was Volchonok, which meant wolf cub) and no one came to my rescue, for my dad was at the front lines fighting, fighting for those children who teased me.

When summer approached, the kindergarten was annexed to a toddler communist organization and we were all taken to a "recreation" camp for a few days. I remember a big dark hall, decorated with red flags. They dressed me in a red tie to the sound of trumpets and a parade of older children along the walls of the hall. The sight was depressing and the atmosphere was morose. I wanted to go home, to be back in that room outside the movie theatre; I wanted to run away from the camp that seemed like prison to me, but I didn't know how. I cried for a few days, until it was all over and I returned home.

It was sad and hard in Stalinabad. Every now and then the city would be shaken by powerful earthquakes and scared people would go out to the center of the street or the empty yards, while their pathetic homes collapsed like a house of cards. Others were trapped inside the buildings and killed. The city was swamped with rumors and horror stories. The grown-ups were talking about a family of Gypsies who was wandering through the streets, putting up tents on the outskirts of town. Every six months the family would return with a new child, usually a baby, and I was told: "A kidnapped child! Be careful; don't hang around them for they will kidnap you too!" The few radios emitted terrible sounds. Every now and then, men wearing uniforms entered the rooms of the refugees around the movie theatre carrying sealed envelopes. Sounds of shouting and cries escaped those rooms when the uniformed men left them. I was afraid of this vision, a terrible and abstruse fear, but this evil reached our doorstep as well. One night there was a knock on the door and two uniformed soldiers stood at the entrance and read from a piece of paper: "In deep sorrow, the Soviet government announces the death of... (the soldier or the officer) ... in the battle of..." Our crying was reserved, but strong enough so that the important details would resonate in my ears. Where did he fall, in the battles of Moscow or Stalingrad, or maybe in a different front? And when did he fall, '42 or perhaps '43?

The artillerymen march was playing somewhere. Was he an artilleryman? Or was he an infantryman or a soldier of the armored forces? And how did he fall? Was it from enemy bullets, a bomb? What kind of a man was he? Where was he born? It all remained unclear to me, for from this moment and for the next forty years my mother never spoke of it and I didn't dare to ask. And so my father was lost to me forever.

A week passed and I walked out of the house. Grandma took me down a long, warm and dusty road, until finally we entered a small black shack where people stood dressed in prayer shawls and prayed. "Synagogue," she told me. "Let's pray for your father's soul." I did not know what that meant.

The terrible visions of war took control over the entire city. Every day a funeral march would move through the main street with coffins for burial. Crying women and children followed the coffins to the cemetery, where they lay flowers by the tombs. I envied these children who could put a flower on the tomb of their father. Months passed; children's fathers returned from the war, or visited on vacation, and brought their sons army uniforms in children sizes, whistles and different gifts, and in the winter they built them sleighs that slid on the snow. And I was left alone and the children's cruelty would hit me without mercy.

August 1984. *The geological tour in Crimea and Caucasus has ended. We are waiting in the airport of a small county town for the return flight to Moscow. I am sitting in the terminal writing a letter: "For the central archive—Soviet Union defense ministry; I would like to find out what has become of a relative, a soldier in the Red Army—Volchonok, who was killed in the big war. Resident of Odessa, he had a wife and a son, an old mother, etc." I signed the letter and tossed it in the mailbox.*

Two years went by before a reply arrived: "The military medical assistant Michael Salomonovitch Volchonok, born in 1914, died from his wounds January 18, 1942. There are no further details."
He was twenty-eight when he died, a young man who did not get to live much. The information matched but was very limited and Mom kept quiet for almost forty years.

ИСПОЛНИТЕЛЬНЫЙ КОМИТЕТ ОРДЕНА ЛЕНИНА
СОЮЗА ОБЩЕСТВ
КРАСНОГО КРЕСТА И КРАСНОГО ПОЛУМЕСЯЦА
103031, Москва, К.Н. Кузнецкий мост д. 18/7   Тел. 221-71-75

При ответе ссылайтесь на наш номер

№ 580050/23   Москва, „ 13 " марта   1986 г.
ДЕЛО:

Красный Щит Давида в Израиле
          г.Тель-Авив

          Уважаемые господа !

     Просим Вас не отказать в любезности сообщить г-ну А.ИТАМАРУ
(адрес прилагается), обратившемуся в Центральный архив Министер-
ства СССР, что, по имеющимся у них данным, военфельдшер ВОЛЧОНОК
Михаил Соломонович, 1914 г.рождения умер от ран 18.0I.1942 года.
Никаких других сведений получить не удалось.
     Заранее Вас благодарим.

          С уважением,   В.П.Фатюхина

                                   Начальник Управления по розыску

ד"א בניסן תשמ"ו
30 באפריל 1986
552/71

                                        לכבוד
                                   מר א. איתמר
                                   המחקר הגיאולוגי הישראלי
                                   מלכי ישראל, 30
                                   י ר ו ש ל י ם

                                   א.נ.מ.,

          בתשובה לפנייתך לארכיב המרכזי של ברה"מ נתקבל
     במשרדנו מכתב מהצלב האדום הסובייטי, בו הם מבקשים להודיעך,
     כי חובש קרבי מר מיכאיל וולצ'ונק ז"ל נפטר מפציעיו ב-18.1.42.
                    רצ"ב תשובת הצלב האדום הסובייטי.

               ב ב ר כ ה,
                   ח. פפירונוב

The letter from the Red Army archives

Chapter Two

"But We Are Going Home Now"

Near the movie theatre where we lived stood a big factory for railway casting. The war and its demands made the factory work day and night, and men and women in overalls would leave at the end of each shift. Mom worked in this factory as an accountant. After a while, she met a Jewish man there, a refugee from Poland who managed to evade the bitter fate of the extermination camps and escape east. Those were hard days for everybody, but mainly for women with children, and it was only natural for a widow to try to find a partner to make the burden of living easier. Feelings and loving memories had no place back then. And, indeed, a year after my father's death, Mother brought the Jewish man who worked at the smithy of the factory home and announced to me and Grandma that she was going to marry him.

Grandma was shocked and enraged; she declared a period of mourning and rejected my mom. She started to have visions and announced that Dad was not dead, but missing, and would be back to avenge his disgrace. Grandma tried to make me side with her. I was torn apart, and at first I did treat the new stranger that entered our house with hostility, but little by little this estrangement filled me with disgust. Grandma moved to live elsewhere and my attitude towards my stepdad became warmer. His name was Shlomo. He was tall and thin with scared eyes, and his attitude towards me was fair and friendly—and a stepdad is not required for more than that, anyway. He would sometimes take me to the factory and show me the work of a blacksmith. There, I saw the white-hot iron tracks coming out of the oven. The noise and the heat were great and my stepdad worked quickly and skillfully. After a while he was ordered to build a new melting oven from scorched bricks, and he performed the task with such quality and speed that he received an award for it and even won the title of "Stachanovitch"—or outstanding employee, which gave its winner both great respect and different privileges.

We enjoyed one of these privileges on "labor day," May 1: we received a small golden apple (which turned out to be an orange) that was cut gently and carefully and divided equally among all family members. It was the first time that I had seen this orange fruit with the strange smell and exquisite taste. On this occasion, around the little orange,

I heard the term "the land of Israel" for the first time; this term was brought up by my stepdad every once in a while and became the subject of vocal arguments between him and my mom.

The sense of family and my personal feelings greatly improved, our economic situation ameliorated, and Grandma reconciled with my stepdad. I started going out more often to the big yard near the movie theatre and onto the street where I befriended several children of different ages. The friendship between children of very different and distant age groups was common in Stalinabad, with the older children serving as guardians to the little ones. I also had one such guardian, a thin and bold boy that was at least five years older than me. He let me ride his sleigh one winter and in summertime he taught me to protect myself against an eye disease that was common among the children during the cotton picking season. The disease, which consisted mainly of unstoppable tears, was caused by the cotton seeds that the wind scattered from the fields in which they grew. The boy taught me to put a urine-soaked handkerchief over my eyes, which was an acceptable means for everyone, and thus one could see during the cotton picking season a crowd of children urinating on their handkerchiefs and then putting them over their eyes.

This new tranquility was disrupted due to several events that followed each other and brought me back to a state of anxiety. My sister was born; she had bright eyes and blond hair, whereas I was dark, almost black. From the moment she was born I felt the outpouring of affection she received not only from my stepdad but also from my mom, and I felt rejected and discriminated against. There was, of course, a great deal of exaggeration in this feeling, for she was a baby and it is clear to everyone that real fatherhood does not resemble a fake one. But as a child I did not possess the required understanding of the situation and my feelings of injustice increased with time. My soldier-dad came back in all his glory; he visited me in my mind. I shut myself off to the world and remained alone with my memories and imagination and became more and more hostile towards my family—and as a result they did the same towards me; for back in those days few parents had a deep understanding of their children's mind.

A blow that befell all of us added more instability and insecurity to my already fragile condition: One night, I heard a noise around the house, but I fell asleep and thought nothing of it. The next morning, we found out that someone had entered our house through a broken window and robbed us of our few possessions—clothes, shoes, boots, kitchenware and food. The blow was hard on all of us. I felt a stinging insult and blamed myself for not paying attention to the noise I heard. I told my mom and stepdad about it and received my share of reproaches from both of them; only my grandma stood by my side, claiming that a child my age could not be expected to discern noises during his sleep. But the sadness, the shame and the guilt were hard to bear and I did not know what to do. The robbing of the food was the hardest blow of all, for these were days of hunger in that land. The food that was sold was rationed, and food that normally would be considered abominable, such as donkey meat, was regarded as edible.

In the meantime, our daily routine, that of the children in the yard near the movie theatre, continued. Every once in a while soldiers would return from the front bringing many gifts, but the most luxurious present that fathers brought their sons was a child-sized soldier uniform, which those lucky children would wear every chance they got. One child, who was particularly arrogant, would walk around the yard showing off his uniform as if it was peacock feathers. The routine continued outside the yard as well, including the mourning parades along the city's main road. But one day, a different parade marched down the street—soldiers and citizens formed a huge crowd; an orchestra of wind instruments played marches, red flags waved and loudspeakers sounded cheers. It was the day of victory over Germany; the war was over; many children's fathers returned from the front. I stood on the street amidst the sounds of joy, but what did I have to do with all of that? I wanted my dad—the triumph and joy were not for me. Then, the arrogant boy approached me with his flamboyant uniform and said with cruelty: "My dad is back—yours will never come back!" I turned around and came back to our little room; I shut the door and windows, sealed my ears and refused to go outside for two days.

Back in those days the arguments over Israel and Palestine increased. My stepdad demanded that we leave Russia and move first to Poland—his birthplace—with the help of his Polish ID, and continue to Israel from there. My mother was opposed to this, but her opposition grew weaker with time. Many refugees were allowed to return to Poland with their Russian wives and their children; the pressure grew stronger and only a small push was needed for us to take that step, which did not take long to arrive.

The image of a policeman in Russia, including Stalinabad, would provoke fear in the hearts of children and grown-ups alike. I remember one day I was walking on the street and an officer in a dark uniform and cap appeared in front of me. I froze in my place; I blushed to the roots of my hair; my heart pounded. The policeman passed by without so much as a glance at me. I ran home where my family barely managed to calm me down. One day I walked the street with my mom and we saw a big brown building around which were many policemen. The fear took a hold of me once more, and this time Mom was scared too. We both moved to the other side of the street and hastily bypassed the police building, and only when we were sufficiently far away did we return to the other side of the road. This was the attitude towards the regular police, but the ones we feared most were the secret police. Horror stories of people being kidnapped in the middle of the night were whispered around. If my stepdad had gone somewhere and was not back in time, my mom would start fidgeting nervously, and the fear—even if it was not explicitly uttered—was known, and one day it turned into a menacing certainty. My stepdad did not return at the end of a work day, did not return all night, nor return the following morning. The house was in a frenzy; Grandma started weeping and crying, and my sister and I sat silently in the corner, confused. The neighbors gossiped quietly and refused to speak to us—talking to the family of a prisoner of the secret police was dangerous. My mom overcame her fear and went to the police office and the office of the Communist Party, but to no avail. In late evening, after 24 hours, he came back and it was as if he came back from the dead; it was a miracle. We sat for a long time listening to his stories about what had happened to him, the investigation and the torture, but his release remained a mystery. We figured that since he bravely withstood the investigation, did not break, and did not sign any papers of confession in his alleged crimes against the state the investigators let him go. It was decided that very evening: We were to leave Russia to go to Poland and move on to Israel from there. The next day we received travel certificates. Mine read: Born in Stalinabad December 6, 1940. Stalinabad was false, so I would be considered my stepfather's child; otherwise I would not be allowed to leave. The December 6 date was correct, but the birth year is shrouded in mystery. Is 1940 correct? Or was I born earlier and I'm one, two or three years older? It is all foggy and burdened with the weight of the tumultuous events whose weight is too heavy for me to bear. The seeds of great moments were sown here, as well as all the evil I had to withstand.

Tel Nordau School in Tel Aviv, fifth grade, 1951. *I was a straight-A student; teachers and students loved me. I was going to a fancy school and studied with Rachel Moreno, one of the most senior and famous teachers. Everybody looked upon me as if I was a shining star, including my family at home. But I was not happy. I was anxious, nervous—I did not understand myself.*

During the summer holiday I went to a summer camp that reminded me of the communist toddler camp in Stalinabad, and I wanted to run home. I suffered there; I met children from circles I did not know existed: slums, transit camps, immigrants from Eastern countries. I returned to school, to the sixth grade, and deteriorated in my studies. I started to mess around in classes and my mischiefs grew more and more frequent to the point when my parents were called for a meeting with the principal. At home, nobody understood how it happened. Only towards the end of eighth grade did I started to recuperate, but the good years had spoiled me—I was accustomed to getting everything with no effort, only now it did not work so well. I failed evening school, and acquired my education at the Beit Bialik library. I asked myself: Were my successes during the first years of pre-school not related to the faking of my age? Was my decline in school later not merely other kids catching up with me and me remaining "stuck" behind? I turned to my mother with a cry and a demanded: "How old am I?! Did you fake my age when we left Russia?!" Mom insisted: "No! You were born in 1940!" and I am not so sure, but the conversation ended immediately. It was not yet time to reveal it all …

In the evening, a farewell party was conducted in the movie theatre for those returning to Poland. An ensemble of singers and actors formed a train structure on stage and sang songs in Polish and Russian, songs of trains that go far, far away, towards home:

Be happy and true
In all that you do,
But we are going home now,
and we bid you adieu.

Lyrics and music: unknown

Translation from Hebrew: Tanya Rosenblit

The next day we boarded an old cargo train from the time of the October revolution, which was carried by a noisy black locomotive with big wheels and a chimney that produced smoke and whistles. We boarded it—the two children, my mom and stepdad. Grandma stayed behind; she refused to leave the country where her son died. "I will die soon," she said. "I have nowhere to go." I cried bitter cries during our farewell—these were my last tears. She was the last memory of my dad.

Chapter Three

"Volga, Volga"

The train was a world by itself. We spent hours, days and even weeks inside it. The train has times of sadness and joy, times of eating and rest, the rising dawn, the sunset and the night. The train has love affairs and quarrels, times of want and times of worry. The wheels of the train are an orchestra of sounds: they play a fast tune and then a slow tune in a varying rhythm. The train honks, groans, squeaks and stops—and melodies accompany it along the way.

The train began accelerating westward. It passed exotic cities: Tashkent, Samarkand, Bukhara... the pinnacles of the mosques protruded above the buildings and walls. People wearing fezzes and wide trousers were seen everywhere, improvised circuses with people walking on stretched ropes were scattered in empty yards. The train traveled fast, making its way through the night as well as during the day, with only short stops along the way. One morning, the view that stared at me from the window was somber and monotonous, a wide desert of sand, rubble and thorny bushes here and there. Heat waves shone above the ground. This was the Karakum, or "Black Sand," Desert, one of the cruelest deserts in the world. From afar one could see a big body of water, bright and steaming. This was Lake Ural. The train turned north from there and continued to slow down, getting slower and slower with time. It would stop and go again, the rhythm changing from time to time. Sometimes it would even back up. Finally, towards the evening, it gained momentum and started galloping forward at full speed. At midnight the train stopped. A mixed smell of water and fuel reached my nostrils. It was a good smell and I fell asleep.

I woke at dawn. Everybody else was fast asleep, and the sun did not shine yet. I peeped through the window—there was a heavy mist outside. Through the mist I saw shadows of cargo wagons and fuel carts, and glimpses of shining and shimmering silver water appeared from between the carts. I dressed and snuck carefully outside; I ran across the tracks and between the carts and reached the beach of the mighty river. The water flowed slowly and quietly—so much so that it was hardly evident that there was any flow at all; small leaves floated on the water. The opposite bank could be seen blurry from afar, and to the south of our bank the buildings and the chimneys of the city were seen as if they were painted on the horizon. It was all dreamy and misty. A lone train worker stepped out to stretch his bones. "Hey mister," I called to him. "What is this?" I pointed to the river. "This is the Volga, boy!" answered the tracker. "And what is this?" I asked, pointing my finger towards the city. "Astrakhan," he answered. And there I was, standing for the first time on the bank of a mighty and tumultuous river and near a city with a mysterious name. I ran back to the train, where everybody was still asleep. I started waking the sleeping with my impatience and excitement: "Volga!" I said. "Volga!" Despite the grumbles and protests everyone slowly woke up, pressed their faces to the window and then stepped outside. The mist had cleared and the river was revealed in its entire splendor; the opposite bank could also be seen clearly. Big and small boats floated on the river; there were also rafts, barges, fishing boats and even one big river ship with a huge chimney, whose toots from its horn would chase away the sleepy tranquility from time to time.

At noon, the train headed north and continued moving along the river for several days. We passed cities, towns and villages; the river ships accompanied us a substantial part of the way as the train ran parallel to the river. The river would change constantly, widening and narrowing; there were forests at its shores at times, and fields could be seen at different times; every now and again small islands would sprout in the middle of the stream. The color of the river would change too—white, then azure then blue.

There were times when it seemed as if we were leaving the river forever and then out of fear and longing for the river I would listen to the ticking of the wheels on the tracks and I'd hear a wonderful melody:

"... Volga, Volga, Mother dear..."

And the train would be back near the riverside.

A big city could be seen from afar. As the train came closer to the city, its pace slowed until we noticed it was no city but a pile of ruins; workers in dusty uniform were clearing the rubble, standing on scaffolds and fixing the ruins. The noise of sledgehammers could be heard; there were also sirens and engine sounds. This was Stalingrad; a city of war, heroism and ruin; many soldiers died here in the bitter and bloody battle. I remembered my father and thought that he might have died here too.

After I received the letter from the Russian Red Cross I wanted to analyze and reconstruct the past. Where was the front in January 1942? Surely it was not Stalingrad, for it was too early still. He might have fallen in Moscow then, or near the Don, or in front of the ruined and burning cities of Kiev and Kharkov. Or maybe in the steppes on the way to Stalingrad? The uncertainty was great and mother was silent. I was filled with an almost religious emotion at the sight of the letter and I wanted to say Kaddish (a Jewish prayer uttered at a funeral) over it, only I didn't know how, and my personal prayer burst out:

Ode to the Combat Medic

Combat medic, thy name shall be praised
While death and darkness did flood;
So far, yet so close to my heart,
Between Moscow and Stalingrad.

What were you doing, brave medic?
In this final and inhumane war;
Did you run through fire and rain?
While the forces retracted some more.

And in that inferno on the riverbank
Was the wounded man screaming your name?
Did you crawl toward him on the snow,
As the little town went up in flames?

Fear not, Michael the medic!
There is no more smoke to behold.
In Heaven, thy name shall be praised:
As the medic who came from the cold.

I remember this medic at spring,
When the train, in pure silence, did pass;
Death and mayhem all lurked on the brink,
And the wind slowly ruffled the grass.

Is this your burial ground?
To be honest, I never could tell.
I'll pray for your soul in the ground,
Peace be upon you, Michael.

Written in 1986, lyrics: Arie Itamar
Translation from Hebrew: Tanya Rosenblit

The train kept moving forward, open-mouthed windows were seen along the way, along with pierced and ruined walls. The sounds of a song—a song of the partisans that fought the enemy—could be heard from afar, in between the ruins:

The fields in the distance were covered in mist,
And the Partisans were preparing.
For battle was approaching inch by inch
With a blood-thirsty enemy daring.

And maybe those same workers that were renovating the ruins are the same warriors that were left from the battle. The train draws away from the ruins and the song disappears along with the rubble. Across the long bridge the train passes the Volga westward and turns into the big Russian steppe.

The steppe is vast, it has fields of wheat, grass, lone trees and groups of trees that protrude from the flat fields, and the trees "travel" in circles in front of the train windows. There are wide oak trees and thin poplar trees with shaking leaves, there are also tall birch trees with white trunks.

The rhythm slowed and the breaks were becoming longer—sometimes they would last 24 hours and more. The passengers' restlessness increased. The nights and mornings were cold, and during the morning hours many passengers would descend hastily from the cars and run with kettles and other containers to fill them with steaming water from the locomotive to use for brewing tea. At one of the stations, while my stepdad ran with the others to fill our kettle, the train started moving. Some of them managed to catch it running, and many were able to climb the rungs as it accelerated, but there were others who were not fast enough and remained on the land; my stepdad was among the latter group. Our anxiety had no limit and the driver of the locomotive did not help. After a few days, the lost passengers appeared sooty as the coal itself, riding on top of an open cargo train that was transporting coal.

The stops and the drives backwards became frequent. During the long stops, we kids would go out and play along the tracks, or in the fields next to it. The summer had just begun and the grain that ripened was the first harvest after the war. Peasant women wearing headdresses would walk around reaping it with sickles. They would sometimes sing sad songs and the Russian steppe would turn into tiring scenery. They would sing a happy song at times and I would listen to the song, to the wind that moved the corn ears and to the train wheels as it all mingled to a chorus:

> *Rise, rise over the fields,*
> *Rise and see the spikes;*
> *... The corn is now ripe*
> *On the sides of the road the grain larks...*

Unknown composers;
Translation from Hebrew :Tanya Rosenblit

The train continued in its back-and-forth movement, northwest and then southwest and then west. It passed the Don River and different cities: Saratov, Kharkov, Kherson..., and their ruins shone from afar. And once again the train reached a vast river—the Dnieper—and from the shore of the river a city with golden cupolas could be seen. This was Kiev—Russia's ancient capital. The train moved northward from there into the marshes and the forests, and the ruined city of Smolensk, in which the partisans fought a war of bravery against the Nazi invader, could be seen from afar.

The year was 1994. *Mom's memory had weakened greatly, but it would wake up every now and then and she would tell me stories: "One day a robber broke into our house... but you don't remember anything because you were little!" And I would continue her story describing each and every piece that was stolen. Mom looked at me with amazement: "How do you remember?!" "I remember," I responded, "and now I want the truth!" Mother looked at me and said: "I knew that someday you would come and ask me." She approached the cupboard and pulled out an old photo of a man. "This is him," she said. "Was his name Michael? Was he a combat medic?" "Yes." "Where did he die?" "Smolensk!" "Not Stalingrad?" I asked with some disappointment. Weird, in January 1942 the front was already far away east of Smolensk and then I remembered the song: "...on the road to Smolensk they marched..." and the picture became clear: The defeated Red Army, in its alarmed pullback east in the* *end of summer 1941, left entire units behind. Many troops remained in the marshes and forests of Smolensk. They slowly organized into partisan units that acted behind the German lines until Smolensk was freed in 1943. Many fairytales were told about the partisans who fought around Smolensk, and I did feel a sense of pride. But why was his place of rest unknown? Maybe it was because of the partisans' fight for survival, the fast moves from place to place, with the Germans on their tail, which led to many of them dying and never being buried or buried hastily with no one remembering their resting place. And despite it all, could it be my mother's imagination?*

The combat medic, Michael, and his wife, Debora.
A wedding photo.

The partisan battles around the city of Smolensk were commemorated in stories and songs; one of them is the unofficial partisan hymn that no one knows when it was composed. My dad could have heard the song and sung it:

The fields in the distance were covered in mist,
And the Partisans were preparing.
For battle was approaching inch by inch
With a blood-thirsty enemy daring.

So said our heroes upon parting:
Here our sons' lives we'll avenge!
And they met face to face in the darkness
While on the road to Smolensk they marched.

They exchanged lead in the woods
Lay him to rest and no one returned,
For the sorrow and sadness were robust,
And the crying in the bitter end—unheard.

Day and night in the hostile surrounding,
The cruel is trembling and running around.
The partisan storm is blowing,
Guiding the sleep of the mourning.

No pair of eyes will see the stranger,
He will not return home.
And through all the mist and danger,
My dear country, I call home.

The Smolensk Partisan Song
Lyrics: Michael Isakowski
Music: Vladimir Zacharov
Translation from Hebrew: Tanya Rosenblit
Translation from Russian to Hebrew: R. Klachkin

The train turned westward towards the Polish border, and we passed the ruined city of Minsk. The sights of destruction became more frequent the closer we came to the border—damaged towns, burned farms and fields, smashed open forests, furniture remains and personal items lying on the road. Soldiers moved eastward in convoys—on foot, in carts, on top of open cargo trains; some of them sang, while others remained silent. Those were the battlefields of Belarus, where millions of people died and families were ruined and lost. Hell peeks out here from every broken window and every cracked wall.

Three weeks after we passed Smolensk, the train arrived at the Polish border. Soldiers and police officers boarded the train and checked certificates, asked questions and interrogated. And I stood there looking back to the big and vast country, my birthplace, for which my father fought and died, but I didn't have anything in common with it. This was a delicate country with beautiful songs, but it was also a cruel and evil place. Farewell my despicable motherland, adieu vast Russian steppe, goodbye fair Volga, farewell you bitter battlefields.

I turned my face; the train moved and entered Polish territory. The refugees of this country started to feel a sense of home. People got off at different stations with their carry-ons, hiring peasants with carts to lead them to their places of residence before the war. They would leave the train with hope mingling with fear: Did something of their homes survive? The train would sometimes not stop at the scheduled places and then whole families would throw their baggage through the openings and jump out of the moving train one after the other; they would then return to collect the piles of stuff along the tracks, put them on their backs and disappear into nowhere.

The train stopped in front of the city of Szczecin on the shore of the Baltic Sea. The former images that I considered hellish were nothing compared to this huge rubble that only Stalingrad could match. There was no whole house, no unperforated wall, and no unbroken window. The wind whined between the ruined houses and sad people wandered here and there among the rubble as if with no purpose. To the side of the track I saw a wooden toy, shattered in part—a dark green bus—and two dolls, one with no limbs. I got off the cart and approached these toys; I looked at them and felt them. I thought of the children that played with them—where were they? Why did they abandon such beautiful toys? Were they escaping? Were they killed in the war? Who were their parents? Would they ever have toys like these again? I did not have the answers to my questions; I just felt sadness and pain. I wanted to cry, but my tears were dry and never returned again.

We continued on our way and we passed an area that belonged to Germany before the war. The remains of scared

German residents were left here and there when the Poles came in and drove their former residents away. A month after we passed the border, the train ride was over and we came to live in a former German town in a small house with an orchard of apple trees. A lonely German woman remained in the house and looked after the orchard. She did not oppose our presence and we treated her fairly and without hatred.

Chapter Four

"Let's dance…"

Two months we spent in the house with the orchard and suddenly an order for movement came from nowhere. We quickly packed our belongings and, with our bags on our backs, stress on our faces and in the air, we boarded a truck. We drove for several hours and then for some reason stepped off the truck and started walking on foot. It was nighttime, and we marched for hours through fields and forests. There was mud on the roads and the lanterns of secluded farms shone from afar.

In the morning we entered a small town and rested in a big empty monastery. I fell asleep and woke up in the evening. We received an order not to leave the monastery so that we would not be seen, but I woke up and snuck outside. I was in a quiet street and saw a white chapel with a bell tower and a cross in front of me. I approached the entrance of the church and heard a melody playing. I went

On foot through the European forests (Davar newspaper)

inside and saw an empty hall with only a piano standing in
its center and a woman sitting and playing it; the woman
did not even look at me. I stood there for a while; the
sounds of the piano were magical and I was mesmerized,
but suddenly the fear awoke inside of me and I returned
to the monastery.

That night we hit the road again, on foot. We formed
a small convoy headed by a man whose authority seemed
great and whose orders were fulfilled quickly. With time,
I was told that it was an emissary from the land of Israel,

from the *Haganah*[1].

The roads were long and hard. My mother carried a big backpack, I carried a small bag and my sister was seated on the backpack my stepdad carried. We crossed fields and forests, we also crossed creeks and half our bodies remained wet for many hours. On the way we met Polish peasants who looked at us with hatred in their eyes; they refused to give us water or food and sometimes they threatened us with their weapons. One night we approached a farm and were greeted with gunshots. The commander of the convoy ordered us to lie down. We lay on the cold wet ground for a while and then we got up and walked on quietly. We slept in secluded barns, and in the fields and forests. We were hungry and thirsty and dogs were set upon us in many places; they would bark at us even from a distance. One night we arrived in a field of beet and kohlrabi and ravished it. I will never forget the taste of kohlrabi, how amazing it was.

Thus we crossed Poland. As we neared the border with Czechoslovakia, the pace grew faster and we started walking during the day as well. Again we were met with hatred by the Polish peasants and their dogs. One of the most common sights on these roads was convoys of refugees;

---

1 *Haganah (Hebrew: "The Defense",* ההגנה *HaHagana) was a Jewish para-military organization in what was then the British Mandate of Palestine from 1920 to 1948, which later became the core of the Israel Defense Forces.*

it turned out we weren't alone. There were many convoys of different nationalities: Russians, Poles, Lithuanians, Tatars and even Chinese traveling east; Italians, Greeks and Yugoslavians were traveling south; only we traveled west. The people in the convoys looked pathetic and shabby, some of them wore the striped uniforms of camp prisoners with meager bundles on their backs, some walked with walking canes and others were handicapped on crutches. They all waved their hands at us excitedly; the word "home" was repeated in many different languages. We also waved our hands—this was a touching "refugee solidarity." And these death camp and labor camp refugees, ex-captives and all sorts of homeless people filled the roads and spread in all directions, searching for the lost home, the city that was no more, the loved ones that would not return to the land of the living. Destruction, suspicion and fear reigned everywhere; but there were three words that stirred hope in all of us: "Land of Israel." The mention of that name electrified the entire convoy, and in my eyes—the eyes of a boy—these words had something mysterious in them, a longing that, if fulfilled, all troubles and torments would be over.

We came closer and closer to the border. After passing a dark and heavy forest the border was in front of us. Polish soldiers inspected everyone carefully, trying to humiliate the people. Their looks were full of hate and our nerves were on end: but cross it! And the passage was like from the land of darkness to the land of light. The landscape remained the same, the forest too, the road as well, but the people! What a difference! The Czech guards were amiable and smiling, the inspection passed easily. We continued marching forward on foot, but the elderly, women, babies and other exhausted individuals were seated on wagons supplied by local peasants. We marched and reached the first Czech border town and I will never forget what happened there.

We walked onto the main road of the town and the windows of the houses opened and a stream of flowers and apples came pouring out upon us. We were hungry and thirsty and we happily gathered the apples and ate them. Did we enter a wonderland? Could it be that people are that good? Was it possible that a barbed-wire fence and a rusty gate—called "border"—separated such different human characters and behaviors? We were told that the name of the town was Náchod. I will always remember the town and its citizens, for what was more important those dark days, after the hate, the shootings and the dogs, than a flower and an apple? I will never forget the somewhat sour, red-green apple, which a woman in a black outfit threw especially at me (so I thought) from the second floor of an apartment building. The apple landed on my shoulder, jumped off and rolled on the road, but one of the members of the convoy grabbed it and gave it to me to eat.

It's very hot, a *khamsin* at the beginning of summer 1962. *I was on a high ladder in an orchard on the kibbutz picking apples. The air was still, flies and mosquitos were humming around us and bothering us, but the landscape was amazing: a green valley, trees, the snowy Mount Hermon on the horizon, fish pools and mountains all around us. And on the tree there were great apples, the first Astrakhan apples to ripen. The past passed through my head again: Astrakhan, the apple in Náchod, the songs in the Russian grain fields... I was picking and eating, picking and eating but to no avail, I was insatiable. Haim the redhead, the orchard coordinator, approached me surprised: "How can you eat so many apples? Do you not have stomach pains?!" There was a hint of a farm man's stinginess that was fighting for every apple for delivery. I laughed: "Nope, nothing hurts." "And how long will you keep eating?" he repeated the question. "Till infinity," I answered, and continued: "The world relies on three things—Astrakhan, Jonathan and Golden Delicious." Haim walked away nodding his head—as if he was dealing with an incorrigible madman.*

And indeed I was mad, mad for apples, and there were apples of many different varieties: Astrakhan was a little tart with a name filled with memories; then there was San Jaquinto, sweet, but a little floury; Pink Lady was big, rugged and oblate; Grand Alexander was very tart but when it ripened it tasted like wine; Landsberg Reinette also had a special winy taste, but it was a wild tree and its treatment was extremely hard; and there was another species called "Reine de Reinettes" that was an orange, firm apple with a delicate taste. "It is an uncomfortable tree," Haim used to say. "The apples don't ripen at once and the picking is hard." But what do I care? I taste, eat and savor every moment. The Czech woman in black in Náchod gave me my first apple, and I have kept eating apples ever since; I am insatiable.

We approached the main town plaza where many youngsters gathered. They were wearing blue shirts, the uniform of the Israeli youth movements, dancing an energetic dance in the Czech town square. "Members of the pioneer youth movements," I was told. They danced and sang:

Let's dance,
Let's swirl...
Ya-lil, ya-lil, ya-lili,
Ya-lil, ya-lil, ya-lili...

Lyrics: Asaf Halevi, music: Arab folk.

It was a simple monotonous song, but it was the first Hebrew song I ever heard, and it had a magic just like the words "Land of Israel." This entire event had an atmosphere of magic and tenderness; the love the people in town gave us, the singing and dancing pioneers. So we remained several weeks in this unforgettable town.

After a long rest we were on the road again, on foot, on trucks and in trains. There was nothing out of the ordinary during our wandering through Czechoslovakia except for one big jolt. We boarded a train near the Austrian border and crossed the border between the world left in ruins and the world that ruined. But the border was ordinary and neither the Austrians nor the Germans guarded it, but rather the Russians—Russian soldiers from the occupation army that remained here.

We stopped in a huge train station with countless tracks that was next to an enormous and quiet river. Trains and wagon parts, carts and locomotors of all kinds were standing on the tracks. We were in Vienna, the capital of Austria, and the river was the Danube. So similar was this image to the Volga and the city of Astrakhan that I was pondering over the meaning of this resemblance when suddenly I heard Russian voices. Russian soldiers with half-naked bodies were running to the water taps laughing and cursing aloud. The grown-ups among us were filled with fear; they silenced the children and forbade us from leaving the train, approaching the soldiers or speaking Russian. They were afraid that the soldiers might suspect that we ran illegally from Russia and might try to bring us back by force. We remained silent with fear, sitting quietly inside the wagons. Then the train moved, with a pace so slow that it was nerve-wracking, but it moved nonetheless. After a few days of journey we passed another border, the Austrian–German border. A lazy and sleepy guard boarded the train and looked to and fro. Authority figures from those that ran the convoys stuck cigarettes, drinks and money into his hands, and it was all over safely. We passed the border into Germany and we saw soldiers again, but they were soldiers of a different kind altogether. The helmets and uniforms were different, the language was strange and weird, and there were black-skinned soldiers among them. It was the first time I saw black people and they seemed extremely similar to the lost sooty-faced refugees from the train in Russia. They were American soldiers that formed the occupation army in most of the south of Germany.

The American soldiers approached us kids, handing out candies, caressing our heads and laughing, but their attempts to make us speak failed. The train continued on and left us in a somber place that was a hard sight for the eyes: a camp with the remains of a barbed-wire fence, long dark shacks, no grass, no trees, no nothing. The streets were paved with protruding pebbles that made walking difficult. The name of that horrible place, according to the adults, was Mauthausen-Gusen. The sight inside the shacks was even more horrible: beds organized in endless rows. We lived with this cruel enemy for two weeks and horror stories about what had happened there not long ago passed from ear to ear. Every once in a while a cry would emerge from one of the shacks or from the yard; these cries were a testimony to the finding of human skeletons, skulls, bones and more, remains of the horrors of the dark days that took place here a while back.

After two weeks we mounted army trucks and traveled away. We reached a beautiful mountainous, woody region; snow could be seen on top of a faraway mountain. We saw a lake on the way; we passed tracks that many trains moved on. We saw many American soldiers, but for the first time German police worked under American supervision. At night we came to a big and crowded camp with many wooden shacks, but they were not long and dark as the ones in Mauthausen. This was the Ainring camp, and we were told, "You will remain here for a while." It was dark outside, but the shacks were illuminated from within. We were carried along the hall and found a vacant room and hurried to camp inside it. There were four beds with mattresses. I lay on one of the mattresses and woke up to a new life, a fixed life of routine with small and pleasant surprises, events and plots, with difficulties and mundane problems, with expectations to the future. The "while" that we were promised to spend in Ainring lasted almost a year.

Chapter Five

"Strengthen the Hands of Our Brothers"

Ainring camp was named after a German town that was located nearby; the entire district was close to the border with Austria. There was another town in the area, Freilassing, where we would visit often, the district capital was Bad Reichenhall, and there was also a very big but faraway city called Munich. The region was known for its beautiful mountain landscape, forests, streams and snow on the mountaintops in the winter. The camp was big and spacious and had empty plains and meadows—a paradise for children's playground games.

Although the adults suffered from unemployment, idleness and the meaningless expectation for the day we would return to the Land of Israel, we, the children, had an interesting and diverse schedule in camp. Our lives were conducted in a triangle: school—youth movement—street and field adventures. School was an exciting experience, for we studied Hebrew and it was the only language spoken in class. I entered the first grade, it was 1946, and thus this year was catalogued, although it turned into 1947. From the beginning I was excited about the strange words and letters; I was a good student and quickly gained full control of the language. (And the doubts tortured me again, for what if my successes weren't but the result of the age difference?) My achievements blinded me and I thought I was special, a feeling that was also nurtured by my parents.

The Hebrew lessons were most fascinating, but with time I understood that the language we learned was an "exile" language that was foreign and strange compared to the *Zabar* (Native Israeli Hebrew) language that was spoken by the people living in the Land of Israel.

In February 1948 *I was accepted into the second grade, although not without a struggle. The principle of the Tel Nordau School in Tel Aviv refused at first. According to him, since I didn't study in the first grade in Israel, and I didn't study at all in the first several months of the second grade, I had to repeat the first grade again, but luckily they decided to test me. I came to school and a strict elderly teacher with glasses on her nose—Shulamit Ben Israel was her name— tested me. She was satisfied, so she smiled at me and said: "The boy knows Hebrew." I was accepted into the second* *grade and the young teacher, whose name was Ivrita, which perhaps was a sign (for Ivrit means the Hebrew language in Hebrew), welcomed me. I was accepted with kindness, as if a red carpet was spread under my feet: "a hero, a ma'apil (an illegal immigrant to Israel), a fighter against the British, a polyglot" and there were other names of honor that I was given. Their Hebrew language was strange to my ears, but so was mine to theirs. I blurted everything I learned in the first grade in Ainring and the kids would burst into laughter, but there was no evil in their hearts. They would correct my mistakes and I would laugh too, but I learned very quickly. Within two weeks I was released from my "exile" Hebrew and learned to speak as a Zabar, although I still had a heavy Russian accent.*

There are stories about new immigrants in the '50s that they and their children were met with hostility by the veterans. Indeed? Then how was I special? Why was I received with so much love and respect? Maybe it was a different time; maybe the tales I told during social-hour class on Fridays about my travels had an impact. The respect the children had for me was enormous, so much so that they turned me into an "arbitrator" on "important" debates regarding politics, super-nations and wars. Obviously, my ruling was unquestioned. I remember one argument where I was asked which nation was stronger—Russia or America. I obviously thought it was Russia, but for some reason I didn't hear the word "strong" and I switched it for "weak" in my head, so

I answered "America," and the pro-American side in class
was overjoyed ... thus I continued to flourish until the sixth
grade.

At the Ainring school I became familiar with Jewish
concepts for the first time: bible studies, Hebrew holidays,
blue-white flag, Jewish history. A large part of the material
was dedicated to the Land of Israel, its landscapes and
what was going on there. Stubborn rumors about war in
the land of Israel circulated between the kids and made
us feel anxious and restless. I heard about a people called
"Arabs" who lived in Israel and fought the Jews. There were
also rumors that there were Arab camps in Germany, much
like Ainring, and they sometimes attacked Jewish camps.

For the Jewish holidays, my parents bought me a very
festive suit: a sailor's uniform. But instead of curiousness
about Jewish holidays, this outfit awakened in me interest
in matters of seamanship, ocean, sailors, pirates and captains. All this without ever seeing a real ocean (assuming I
never saw or I don't remember the sea in Odessa). I learned
how sailors looked according to their positions and ranks
from books, but with time I understood that this kind of
"education" was of little value.

A sailor's uniform for the holidays

The youth movements in Ainring were an impressive and graceful phenomenon. They were directly copied from the factional partition in the adult world. My entire life in the camp had been conducted through factions, and there were many of them: right-wing to left-wing parties, as well as some religious factions. The division of money, immigration passes to Israel, food stamps, as well as different benefits was done via the party centers, and they had the last word. There were plenty of arguments among the adults about political issues and we kids witnessed parts of these angry arguments without understanding a thing. Yet for us the equivalent partition into youth movements was

not accompanied by arguments and hate, but by natural competition between children belonging to different groups. Another phenomenon that characterized the youth movements in Ainring was that very small children from the age of six were accepted to the different groups.

My father, who was an activist in a Zionist left-wing party, naturally directed me to the Dror—*HaMahanot HaOlim*[2] youth movement. It was an elated feeling to come almost every evening to the club, play checkers and other games, sing, listen to beautiful stories, stories about the Land of Israel, and celebrate interesting holidays, such as Chanukah.

The first grade pupils had a particularly exciting ceremony: our official acceptance to the movement. There was a stage in a big hall decorated with white-and-blue flags and red flags. Photos of very important people hung behind the stage. Behind a table on the stage sat people who apparently deserved a lot of respect. My instructor—Gita was her name—was a kind, fat and tall girl, who constantly wore a blue *sarafan*[3]; she escorted me onto the stage. Behind my back were the important people and the photos, on both

---

2 *HaMahanot HaOlim is a youth study group with Zionistic and socialistic philosophy to be founded in Israel. Since its inception in 1929, members of HaMahanot HaOlim have continually worked to promote a wide range of projects that benefit Israeli society. There are currently over fifty branches throughout Israel and over 7,000 members.*

3 *A sarafan is a traditional Russian long, trapeze-shaped jumper dress (pinafore) worn as Russian folk costume by women and girls.*

sides of the stage were the flags and below the stage was a big crowd who was watching me. I was excited because of the grandeur of the event and my face beamed. The instructor tied my tie and attached the symbol of the movement to my shirt and I, enthusiastically, raised my right hand and curled it into a fist with two fingers protruding in the air. With these fingers I swore allegiance to Dror—HaMahanot HaOlim and repeated the slogan "We shall arrive to the Holy Land" with the crowd repeating after me and cheering. The instructor kissed me and I felt on top of the world. Then everybody got up on their feet and sang different hymns, one of which I particularly liked:

> *O Strengthen the hands of our brethren,*
> *Who, though scattered far and wide, cherish the soil*
> *of our homeland,*
> *Let not thy spirits fall, but with joy and song,*
> *Come shoulder to shoulder to the aid of our nation.*

Birkat Ha'am
Lyrics: Haim Nachman Bialik
Music: unknown
Translation from Hebrew: Tanya Rosenblit

There were red flags, symbols and ties—like in the toddler camp in Russia, but there was such a difference in the atmosphere. In Russia there was somberness, fear, discomfort; here there was elevated spirits and excitement.

The acceptance ceremony for the Dror—
HaMahanot HaOlim movement

Lag BaOmer[4], 1952. *A year before I was accepted to the HaShomer HaTzair[5] youth movement. On this day we were*

---

4   *Lag BaOmer (Hebrew: ל"ג בעומר) is a Jewish holiday celebrated on the thirty-third day of the Counting of the Omer (According to the Torah (Lev. 23:15), we are obligated to count the days from Passover to Shavu'ot. This period is known as the Counting of the Omer.), which occurs on the 18th day of the Hebrew month of Iyar. According to the Talmud and Midrash, this day marks the hillula (celebration, interpreted by some as anniversary of death) of Rabbi Shimon bar Yochai, a Mishnaic sage and leading disciple of Rabbi Akiva in the 2nd century, and the day on which he revealed the deepest secrets of Kabbalah in the form of the Zohar, a landmark text of Jewish mysticism. In modern Israeli culture, the holiday has been reinterpreted as a commemoration of the Bar Kokhba revolt against the Roman Empire.*

5   *HaShomer HaTzair (Hebrew: השומר הצעיר, translating as The Youth Guard) is a Socialist–Zionist, secular Jewish youth movement founded in 1913 in Galicia, Austria-Hungary, and was also the name of the group's political party in the Yishuv in the pre-1948 British Mandate of Palestine .*

at a camp in Heftsiba Forest near Hadera. I was excited for it was the day when I was about to receive the badge of the movement and the green tie of the junior league. I walked around the eucalyptus forest, which was so different from the forest in Ainring. It was much brighter and hotter. There was an exciting game of two flags at night. I was running through the forest, hiding, raising the flag, "becoming captive," "being released"—there were countless experiences. The day before, we walked along the beach from Hadera to Caesarea. How magical was the sea, the sunset, the ancient pier of the ruined city, the clean sand ... and we sang Hannah Szenes's song "Walk to Caesarea."

And indeed, a year before, when I enlisted in the movement, I was received with honor, like in the second grade of Tel Nordau School. My biography, Exodus, Russia was very significant to the kids of HaShomer HaTzair back then. But it was difficult for me since I was a stranger and strange I was in society, an unpopular child. My parents also burdened me; they were afraid of the government that was opposed to HaShomer HaTzair; like in Russia, they were afraid for their income and forbade me from going. I defied them and went in secret, shoving the blue shirt into my pocket and putting it on in the stairwell and then taking it off before entering the house. I was faithful to the movement and despite my estrangement I loved the atmosphere. The fact that I had to sneak into the meetings increased the respect the other kids had for me.

I received the tie and symbol, once again raised my two fingers enthusiastically like back in Ainring and repeated the slogan three times: "be strong and brave." A different place, a different movement, a different slogan, but still: the same blue shirt, the same fingers, the same atmosphere. But, really, why did I go to HaShomer HaTzair and not to Mahanot Haolim?

Some of the most important experiences in the youth movement in Ainring were the parties that were dedicated to Hebrew holidays, which were completely new to me. One evening, at the end of winter, when it was still snowy, I walked to the club like I always did, when suddenly two ghostly and frightening figures appeared from the darkness, covered in white sheets. One of them had a skull-like head which I found to be very scary, and the other one resembled—according to the descriptions I heard from different rumors—an Arab. They attacked me shouting in scary voices. I started calling out for help and running, but no one heard me. I barely got away from the two and reached the club. I ran to the instructor and told her that two demons attacked me and that we needed to call the police. She responded with a smile and let me into the main hall where, to my surprise and amazement I saw the two "demons" and many other funny and scary characters dressed in colorful outfits and masks. I was stunned, but I was beginning to slowly understand that this was some kind of a celebration. This is how I was introduced to Purim (a Jewish holiday that commemorates the deliverance of the Jewish people in the ancient Persian Empire from destruction in the wake of a plot by Haman, a story recorded in the Biblical Book of Esther).

After Purim, there was Passover. I heard stories about the holiday and its meaning, and the camp was preparing a big celebration that was scheduled to take place after the holiday feast (*Leil Haseder*). My dad was an active participant as one of the actors in the company that was supposed to put on a play based on life in the camp, using symbols from the Haggadah. The long-awaited day arrived and I dressed in my festive sailor's uniform and went to the movie theatre in the camp with my mom, sister and many neighbors. Actors, singers, entertainers and magicians got onto the stage one after the other and demonstrated their wonders. Finally the part of the show my dad was in. I don't remember much of it, but one part remained engraved in my memory: a big piece of cardboard with animal paintings was placed on the stage, with holes the size of a human head in different places on it. When a cue was given the holes were filled with human heads, each of which represented the head of one of the cartoon animals. Soon enough I recognized my dad "peeping" from the head of a deer. I started shouting and calling out to him from the audience, to the laughter of the people. My dad returned a wink and made a face. All of a sudden all the heads burst out singing: "One little goat, one little goat ... which my father bought for two zuzim" ("Chad gadya, chad Gadya, dizabin abah bitrei zuzei"—a famous holiday song). During the song my dad kept looking and winking in my direction, to my utter delight.

The third part of the kids' daily routine was the adventures on the street and in the field. Every day, after school, a group of kids of different ages would gather and go look for adventure. One of our mischiefs was going to the Austrian-German border and provoking the guards. They, knowing we were Jews, were afraid to respond to our teasing. There were rumors that armed fire-teams of Jewish soldiers from the allied forces were looking to kill Germans and Austrians, perhaps as a revenge for what happened in the war or as a response to provocation against Jews. We walked through the mountains as well; we reached a fortress that was said to be Hitler's house. We would play hide and seek, tag and other playground games in the woods and the meadows. Sometimes we would conduct a "visit" in the German town Ainring and enter a pub or a beer house. The older children among us would mimic the American soldiers, sitting down in a cocky fashion on the chairs, raising their feet up on the tables and commanding the elderly German waiter in an authoritative tone to serve everyone some beer. He would quietly obey and do what he was told. The Germans that lived in the area were filled with fear and stress, they all whispered quietly and we felt we were their masters. Of course, it never occurred to us to actually pay for the beer.

One of our most daring exploits could have ended in tragedy. Ainring was a region with heavy train traffic 24 hours a day; there were civilian trains, cargo trains and American military trains. Along the track every few kilometers were underground trenches closed with iron doors. These trenches caught our attention for a long time, until we finally decided to enter one of them and see what was inside. We approached one of the trenches, lifted the iron cover and a spectacular view revealed itself to us: phone wires, tubes, switches, buttons and other types of technological equipment we did not understand. We went inside and started playing with the switches and cutting telephone tubes from their cables. Because we liked the tubes we each took one. And so, happy and excited, we left the trench and went towards camp. Along the way we noticed a strange turmoil among the Jewish police officers who were in charge of the camp, American military officers, German officers and rail authority officials in blue caps. They then spotted us with the tubes. At once, this diverse crowd ran to us and the camp police officers sat us on the sidewalk and started interrogating us as a big crowd from among the camp tenants stood around listening. Out of our naivety, we told them what we had been doing in the trenches without understanding what the whole commotion was about. When the interrogation was over, our parents were summoned and one of the camp leaders gave a moving speech in which he called our actions "hooliganism." He explained that what we did not only damaged the property of the rail authority, but worst of all damaged the rail company's communication center and paralyzed all the traffic in the area, and that it was a miracle that there were no train collisions. The man complained about the damage and shame we caused the image of the people in the camp "and in Germany of all places." We were punished with a week of detention during which we couldn't leave our houses. We also promised that we wouldn't leave the camp without an adult in the future, and that we wouldn't repeat these kinds of tricks. After the train incident the group's gatherings after school hours became scarce.

Another incident that was particularly uncomfortable was the periodic disinfection against mice that was performed every few months. The shacks teemed with mice and the only way to get rid of them was by sealing them shut and killing them with tear gas. On disinfection day some belongings needed to be taken out of the shack, the remainder was wrapped in fabric and paper, the windows were closed and we waited 24 hours until the gas smell faded to return. Disinfection day was a big fuss for adults, since on top of it all we also needed to spend the night with friends or relatives, but I liked it because we always stayed with the family that lived in the neighboring shack; they had a daughter I was in love with. Her name was Dvora'le, she had dark skin—almost like a gipsy—and a pair of dark flaming eyes, but she was a few years older than me.

Tragic events took place in the camp as well; I remember one in particular, when on a Saturday a truck that drove people from the camp to a soccer game in the neighboring camp turned over. There were a few dead and several wounded. Camp Ainring was in heavy mourning after this incident.

At times the movie theatre played movies in the camp; my parents took me to see one that I remember in particular, an Italian film about the anti-Nazi underground. There I heard the concepts "Nazi" and "anti-Nazi" for the first time. I didn't understand much of what was going on up on the screen (the movie had no subtitles), but I felt the movie's somber atmosphere and I remember it well. One tragic bit remains engraved in my memory: a man, the protagonist, was climbing up dark stairs with a lit oil lamp, a morose melody accompanying his ascent, the dark night surrounding him with only the light from the lamp to see. Soldiers in dark uniforms and belts with shining buckles followed him to the roof. The man stood in front of the soldiers, lamp in hand, teasing them with defying cries. The soldiers raised their weapons and started firing, the man collapsed and fell, the lamp fell on the ground but remained lit, and a woman appeared from nowhere, rushed to the man's body and burst into tears. I went to see this movie several times to try and understand it, until I understood some of the plot: It was a movie about an underground resistance that fought against the Germans and the Italian fascists. The man, the leader of the resistance, was caught and executed, apparently due to the betrayal of his beloved—the woman who cries at the end of the film. I have a clear view of the image of the man with the oil lamp and I can still feel the bleakness and sadness of the scene, but I don't remember the melody.

The concepts "Nazi" and "anti-Nazi" returned when an old German man from the neighboring village came to visit us. The man's name was Schumacher; he was fat, short, and wore suspenders and leather pants, a felt hat and glasses. He was a locksmith and he would come to the camp to do different jobs, mainly fixing locks. He often visited us and my parents treated him with kindness and friendship. The man had a kind look in his eyes and I liked him, despite all the bad feelings against Germany and Germans. For some reason I couldn't connect Schumacher to the atrocities done by the Germans. My parents later told me that Schumacher was an "anti-Nazi" and that he, too, suffered during the war.

September 1976. *I was back in Europe for the first time for an advanced study class, in Austria of all places, close to the border with Germany, not far from the gate where we used to tease the guards. Thirty years had passed since that time. The landscape remained similar, the tall mountain range where Hitler hid, according to rumors, remained almost the same. I went to the old border crossing, but nothing* *remained. I returned to Germany for the first time in 1987, after forty years. I was nervous before the plane landed but in one moment all the stress disappeared. The people seemed completely ordinary, nothing remained from the Ainring views of the past; it was still Germany, but a totally different place. I arrived in Heidelberg, an ancient city with a green river, churches, historic buildings, a pedestrian street and an imperial palace on a woody mountainside. I walked through the forest that surrounded the palace; I was told that the founding conference of the Nazi party was held in this forest. I felt like I was the only living being walking among the skeletons of the first Nazis. The people seemed ordinary to me, the adults looked like Schumacher, the locksmith. Could they be the same individuals who committed these atrocities?*

The end of the school year was approaching and intense preparations for the graduation party were taking place. As the "star of the class" I had to read two verses from a Hebrew textbook at the party. The first one was:

Oh what a shame
For an apple that befell,
It fell from the tree top,
Fell and popped...

The second was a verse of which I remember just the first three words: "The bally ball..." and next to it was a picture of a child playing ball. I prepared a lot for that party and memorized both verses, but when the moment arrived and the graduation party with all the many participants took place, I confused the words a little, and to make things worse, another boy read the same verses, only he was in 6th grade. And despite it all, the teacher consoled me and said that my oration was better than that other boy's. The higher classes presented beautiful plays and the choir sang songs—all in Hebrew. We had our picture taken for the class yearbook.

The party was held two days before the end of the school year. Two days after that I was supposed to receive the yearbook photo and my diploma and thus finish a slow and relaxed year in a normal and orderly fashion. I was expecting another similar year, when suddenly everything changed. No more slowness and routine. A time of calm had ended and tumultuous and rough times returned, where events raced one after the other and changes would appear within days or even hours.

After the exciting yet tiring day of the party I went to sleep. None of us knew what that special night of June 1947 had in store for us. I awoke because of a loud noise in our living room. There was turmoil and bewilderment, Dad was packing, my sister was crying, two people were walking around nervously rushing my parents. One of them put a big camera on a tripod and Dad hung a big white, creased sheet on the wall. They sat us down one by one in front of the sheet, and the man with the camera flashed photos. I was half asleep wearing a wrinkled pajama shirt, sitting and staring in front of the sheet as the photographer took pictures.

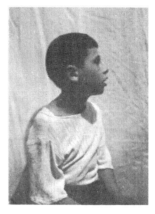

"Passport" photo for sailing on The Exodus

They dressed me while I could barely stand on my legs, and then slowly they started to explain to me what was going on: "We are going to the Land of Israel." These words electrified me again, words I almost forgot during the calm period. I started to work fast as well. They explained that the photograph was needed for the preparation of a passport (fake, of course) to cross the European borders and reach the port from which we should sail to Israel; it would serve to mislead the British who controlled parts of Germany and the Land of Israel and who opposed Jews entering the country. I was given a strange name—Greek, maybe—and I was ordered to memorize it by heart and answer at each border crossing to this name alone and to no other. I was forbidden by all means to speak or utter any words in Hebrew, Yiddish or Russian; it was said that the best thing to do was to shut up. The dawn has risen; I was rushed to school to receive my diploma and the year-book photo. There were only a handful of children who won the bliss of going to the Land of Israel and I was the only one from my class. The children who saw us leave were jealous and said that "Israel is at war ..." but I could care less. I boarded the truck (of the American forces, it seemed) happy and thrilled. The truck took off and we were on our way.

Yearbook photo of the first grade in Ainring that started at the end of 1946 and ended in 1947

Chapter Six

"Between Mountains and Borders"

While the truck was moving on the road, I was thinking about the incomprehensible changes of time. First, traveling in slow trains that go to and fro, drive one day, rest two days and so on; then gruesome and dangerous journeys on foot, and after almost a year of calmness and tranquility, we're suddenly on such a hasty move again. I asked my parents what it all meant but they couldn't explain it. The leader of the convoy, a guy from Israel, smiled when he heard my questions and answered only this: "You are going to the Land of Israel." After a hile I understood the meaning of it all: a big ship with a capacity of thousands had been purchased in the United States and was on its way to Europe to take in *Ma'apilim*[6] to Israel. These thousands

---

6 *Ma'apilim - Illegal immigrants who came to Palestine in the Aliya Bet program before and after World War II (The Encyclopedia and Dictionary of Zionism and Israel).*

of passengers needed to be transferred to the ship at once; the passengers were chosen from the camps that were scattered around Germany and we were among the winners.

The road passed a calm German landscape. In the villages and small towns no signs of war could be seen, but in the big cities the signs were more obvious. We passed through Munich, a giant city with a lot of ruins. There were more ruined cities along the way, but they could never compare to the spectacle I witnessed in the city of Szczecin, in Poland.

We passed a few borders inside Germany—borders that separated the occupied ally territories: the American region, the British region and the French region. There was a lot of tension in the British region. The calling of names in these checkpoints was done mechanically, and the cigarette packets, the dollars and the wine bottles that were given to the guards made the process easier, but there was still much tension. Once I forgot to answer to the funny name I was given and received some shoves in my ribs as a result, which didn't help either, until finally my dad answered for me. The grown-ups gave me severe looks but didn't utter a word.

Finally, we arrived at the French border. Again, the stepping off from the truck, again the name calling—and here we are in France. At night we arrived at a huge train station in the city of Strasburg, where we were kindly greeted by good people and elderly women who served us fresh and tasty food. The people and the women were from the *Jewish Joint Distribution Committee* (JDC or *Joint*), the Jewish organization that helps refugees, and the *United Nations Relief and Works Agency* (UNRWA). After we dined, people from both organizations started handing us clothes. There were different kinds of clothes that had been donated from people around the world: evening gowns, elegant tail suits, coats, blouses, hats of all shapes and colors, belts, ornaments, socks and whatnot. My parents picked different things for me and my sister while I picked two: a felt pilot's hat which had an intense green color and ear protectors, and a thick belt made of leather with diamond-like colorful glass beads. I don't know what happened to my taste in fashion back then... but still, I remember looking after these two possessions as they traveled with me all the way, through land and sea, and together we arrived in the Land of Israel.

The year was 1956. *I was 16 years old and was about to receive my identification card. I wanted to be a zabar, a native Israeli. A long time ago, weeks after I arrived to Israel, I parted ways with my pilot's hat, when I realized that it looked ridiculous to the zabars. I held on to the belt for longer—but it wore away as well and I threw it out—but I couldn't get rid of what was inside. I stopped speaking Yiddish; I hated that language which to me symbolized exile. I got rid of my Russian 'R' and took on a zabar accent—but* *inside I remained different. I mercilessly, and without any understanding, attacked the behavior of the Jews in the holocaust, their seemingly passive walk towards death. I could only identify with the rebellion of the ghettos and, of course, with the soldiers who fought the Nazis. I hurt my stepdad. I was nourished and fed by heroic paratrooper stories, the 101 (a famous commando unit that operated in the 1950s), heroic retaliation stories and the memory of two instructors who died in battle. I waited anxiously for my enlistment in the army. I had physical problems, but I wanted to be a zabar like everybody else, and I overcame everything due to my willpower and became a paratrooper— but I was still different. I participated in wars and even displayed acts of courage every now and then—but inside I was different, heavier; heavy from the burden of memories and the abundance of events.*

In the morning, we were on the trucks again. "Where to?" we asked the head of the convoy. "To *Mizra* (code name for the area near Marseille, France)," he answered. No one knew what Mizra was. After a tiring day and night we reached a forest and in the forest there was a white castle with long windows—this was Mizra. In fact, it was a secluded farm in the forest that was rented especially for us. Again we unpacked our belongings and again we all lived in one room. The next day we were to continue on our way to the sea where we were to board a ship and I was excited in anticipation of this, but this was not what happened. We got up in the morning, we were handed food and drinks, and then nothing happened. Everybody was concerned, waiting and waiting, and there was no one to talk to. One of the people in charge appeared in the evening and asked everyone to be patient for he didn't know how long we would have to wait, but he unequivocally promised us that we were on our way to Israel and that the day we would board the ship was close. Thus started another episode of routine and mundane life peppered with small and insignificant events. While we kids would play in the forest, have fun and waste time, and while young lads would go out to the forest in secret, practice with their weapons and come back with a mysterious smile on their lips whispering Haganah—while all this was taking place, above our heads a great battle was unfolding. So I was told after several years, about the political, diplomatic and intelligence battle over the fate of the ship that was supposed to receive us on board, and about our own destinies. The British Empire, the Jewish Agency, the Haganah, the French, the Americans, the Italians, the Russians, the Arabs, diplomats, secret agents, reconnaissance and intelligence planes, war ships and whatnot—all participated in the battle. This was the reason for the delay in our boarding the ship that escaped its persecutors in search of a safe harbor for us to board. But we didn't know a thing of all this and we kept on playing.

During our wandering around the farm area, we ran across an old French lady who would carry potato bags from the fields to the farm. We would tease her and scorn her and call her "gentile." I didn't understand the meaning of that word, but the way we treated her made me sad and angry. I would approach her and help her carry the potato bags. One time she led me to some dark alcove which was furnished with a bed, a table and a small oil oven for cooking. On the way to the alcove, as well as in the alcove itself, she talked to me in a language I didn't understand. I tried to speak to her with hand gestures, but to no avail. I consoled myself with the fact that I helped her carry her bags. While she was talking, she suddenly started crying, and then she started kissing and caressing me, taking a small tied handkerchief from the table drawer. She untied the knot and pulled three faded photographs from the handkerchief. There were three beautiful and strong young men: the first in a farmer's uniform with a straw hat and a moustache, the second shaved and wearing a fancy suite, and the third dressed in an elegant army uniform. Every time she drew my attention to the photos, she crossed herself and cried, and through her crying she constantly repeated the words "La guerre"—the war. I felt bad for this old woman who lost three sons in the war and was now living on her memories while walking around with a bag of potatoes, among children who harassed her. I remembered my father who was killed in battle, the wounded soldiers and the abandoned toys near the city of Szczecin.

While we were biding our time, another sudden order for movement arrived. The packing was fast and at sundown we were on the trucks and on the road again. Peeping through the canvas covers I saw a huge convoy of trucks suddenly assembling from nowhere. There was a heavy fog, the roads were quiet and silent and the huge convoy was moving lazily on the tricky side roads. Every once in a while we would stop, go, stop again and then go again. The rocking of the truck put me to sleep and the sun shone on me in the morning. I got off the truck and the boundaries of my imagination back then were not wide enough to take in the image that unfolded in front of my eyes: a light blue sea and endless water, till the end of the horizon. Up to that moment I remembered only the images of a two-sided river, but here there was no shore at the far end of the horizon. A small white town resided on the bay coastline. It was a hot day and a misty vapor was rising from the water. On the shore, tied to the long pier, stood a ship that looked like a huge monster out of fairytales. The ship had three decks with three balconies surrounding them, countless windows, a huge chimney in the middle, ropes, cables, white lifeboats, floats. It seemed the ship was made of wood.

One after the other, the trucks arrived at the pier, unpacking their human cargo, and the crowd organized in a row; a long and excited human-snake was twisting on the pier, many excited but controlled individuals marched in queue and in perfect order to the vessel wall and, from there, climbed the wooden gangplank into the belly of the ship. There were men, women and children, but the majority were members of youth movements and large groups of parentless children from orphan houses. They were all marching and singing unstoppably: songs of hope, songs of bravery, songs of war and struggle:

Between mountains and borders
In starless nights—
We accompany endless convoys of brothers
To our homeland filled with light

For the newborn—
We'll open the gate
For the old man—
We are the fortress, here we stand.

The unofficial hymn of the clandestine immigration
Lyrics: Haim Hefer, music: V.A. Agapkin
Translation from Hebrew: Tanya Rosenblit

This was one of many songs the children in the youth movements and orphan houses sang; the marching crowd joined them on their way towards the ship. And me—the little boy standing on the pier, listening, watching, being impressed, excited and yet not realizing that I was living and breathing one of the biggest and most exciting human events of all times. I boarded the ship.

A young group the likes of which I had never seen before welcomed us on board: guys with huge forelocks, short pants and sloppy clothes; girls with long braided hair who at times were also dressed in sloppy clothes. One of the guys turned and spoke to us in Hebrew, in a style that was foreign and weird to my ears, and led us and a few other families along the middle balcony of the ship. He opened the door and a room was revealed to us—in fact, it was a small cabin with bunkbeds. Four families entered the cabin, each family received a bunk and was forced to huddle together "until we reach Israel," said the guy, "Make it work." We did. Who even cared about the crowding and the conditions—in this special atmosphere of elated spirits and sanctity, there was no room to think about the hardships. The young people from the Land of Israel continued to pass and visit the cabins, chat, encourage, and tell stories of the Land of Israel. Little by little we got used to their sloppy clothing, their free and blunt habits and the way they talked. All of us—including me—looked at the young guys with admiration and respect. They were the mariners and the commanders that were supposed to lead the ship; they were from the Haganah, Palmach, and Palyam (guerrilla organizations that fought the British occupation), the best of the Jewish youth on a rescue mission for thousands of refugees who were wandering around Europe.

It was evening; the day had worn me out and I fell soundly asleep. We all slept quietly and safely that night, but a hectic and nervous activity was taking place around us. The leaders of the world continued to deal with the destiny of the ship and its chances to embark. The chances were slim, we were told—the ship was not allowed to leave the port. But those young men overcame all the difficulties, outwitted the harbor authorities, lifted the anchor and set sail in the cover of the night to the open sea. When the morning came, I found myself surrounded with water and light was flickering over the waves. I didn't know what it was, as it was the first time I saw such a sight. It looked like liquid gold was flowing on the water, and only my parents' explanation led me to understand that it was the reflection of the sun in the sea. I fell in love with the sea.

August 1949. *I had been sitting on the beach for hours looking at the blue-green water, the white waves, the sand and the old Tel Aviv pier. Sometimes I would lie inside the warm water from morning till evening. Every morning I would wake up, go onto the balcony, and watch the sea. The sea surrounded me when I was coming and leaving, during the day and during the night. Later, after a few years, I'd sit on sand and limestone hills that steeply descended to the beach. The evening primrose on the shore covered the hill. It was dusk and a sailing boat appeared on the horizon. I was sitting and painting—I painted the sea in the morning, at night, at sunset and at sunrise, in calm and torment. The paintings were all lost save one, but the images remained traced in my memory. I saw books, paintings in exhibitions, and I was always looking for the sea and the ships. I repeatedly read all the travel stories: Magellan, Vasco da Gama,*

Columbus, Captain Cook, the Mutiny on the Bounty, etc. I cherished a dream to sail the ocean and reach the southern islands. I saw movies about pirates, storms, remote islands. I had an atlas since I was a child, from which I would copy islands and faraway oceans. My parents were not pleased with this occupation and forbade me from practicing it fearing it would "interfere with your studies," as they put it. So I continued practicing it on Saturdays and in the mornings under my blanket.

Every morning I would go onto the balcony, look at the sea and say: today will rain... it will rain in the evening... today will be a beautiful day... today will be hot.... I knew to feel the sea and interpret its secrets. This is the same sea I fell in love with on July 7, 1947, when I saw it for the first time from the deck of the ship.

Chapter Seven

"There Will Remain
One of the Captains"

As the sunlight was jumping over the waves and we kids ran around in excitement between the decks, the rooms and the ropes of the big ship, a persistent murmur appeared from above. Finally there appeared the shadow of a plane that circled several times over the ship and then disappeared. Stress and anxiety spread throughout the decks. Some passengers told us it was a British military airplane that had discovered us prematurely; they told us that we were supposed to arrive at the Israeli shores in secret.

During the first day of sailing, the young Israelis explained the ship to us—where it was purchased, how it came to shore, about illegal immigration, about the Brits who block the ways of Ha'apala ships and about the deportation of the Ma'apilim to Cyprus, which is near Israel. But they had a profound faith that we were going to break the quarantine and arrive ashore safely. They told us that the Brits wouldn't dare to stop such a big ship with so many people. And if they tried to stop us, there were only a few kilometers in the middle of the sea that were "territorial waters," and in the little time they had they wouldn't be able to succeed and the ship would manage to overcome the attempts to stop it and arrive ashore. They told us that the fact that the ship was discovered today didn't change a thing. Their words inspired us with confidence and faith, but there was one thing those naïve boys didn't take into consideration: all the information about the size of the ship, its capabilities and its ability to overcome short-term obstacles—this was all known to the Brits too.

During the afternoon hours, two big banners were hung on the ship, one in Hebrew and one in English, which read "Exodus." A blue-white flag was hung on the stern. We memorized the name of our ship without realizing it would become an exciting historic symbol.

We kids quickly learned that in the middle of the ship, in its interior, was a radio apparatus that broadcast messages and songs. One by one, many children and even some adults, including my father, gathered on the spot; we sat on the wooden floor listening to the broadcasts. Some of the broadcasts were in the spoken languages among the Ma'apilim—Yiddish, Polish, Russian—but most of the broadcasts were in Hebrew. Occasionally, the speakers uttered words we didn't understand that were probably codes and secret messages to the forces that were awaiting our arrival along the shores of Israel. The broadcast would start like this: "Telem, Shamir,, Boaz—this is Exodus" and then the radio uttered phrases and names like "the white book," "Haganah," "combat," "rebellion," and more. Many songs were heard on the radio: "Among stormy waves to those who carved their ways"; "a ship scouts in secret," which was a song that became a hit during all seven days of sailing; "blue waters of the sea—fair Jerusalem." "There will remain one of the captains" was a particularly loved song because it reminded us of a popular figure on the ship—the captain:

In the wintery night the light was flickering,
The anchor was squeaking afar.
The sea was black. A person said quietly:
"Two more boats and again we're alone."

There will remain one of the captains,
And the seamen—they were three.
He told them: "Let's sail to the distance,
Starry night shines over the village, see."

The sea is an abyss with endless depths to explore.
Waves will hit the rocks while we sail on and on.
There is but a hint of the memory of the distancing land,
From the illegal ship we look forward ahead.

He was a simple man with no stars or shine,
His chest was bare and he had blue eyes.
His friends were out there in the underground,
His friends were lying on the ground.

But "13" and from the night again,
We'll toast the anchor and flags.
They will anchor at daylight, friends,
And the singing of the clandestine immigrants will be
raised.

Until then, we silently pick up our rows,
Upon the captain's command
Mother, the captain says hello,
And sets sail to the west once again.

The Captain's Song

Lyrics: Haim Guri, music: Russian folk

Translation from Hebrew: Tanya Rosenblit

One of the strangest sights in my eyes was that of the captain of the ship. I got used to the guys and girls who held our destinies in their hands; they looked like beggars, with their way of speaking, dressing and behaving that didn't resemble that of fearless warriors or tough seamen, and certainly not the cruel, scarred-cheek pirates the Brits later depicted them as. But the sight of the captain was beyond any image I had in my mind about such a character. And the following was how I saw him for the first time.

One day, a young guy in sandals appeared on the central deck, near the radio; he was about 25 years old. He had a huge forelock, and wore short khaki pants with the hems carelessly folded up and long puffy pockets dangling loosely on his legs. He wore a white shirt with one side tucked in his pants and the other sticking out. To me, it was the symbol of the Zabar, the Israeli Palmach warrior, but then I saw everyone getting up on their feet, children and adults alike, making way for him to pass through the crowd, looking at him with respect and admiration and whispering "Kapitan"—Captain. It was the first time in my life that I saw a real, live, flesh and blood captain, but his looks were so different from anything I had seen in picture books. To me, the image of a captain was that of a big, tough man with a beard, dressed in a dark blue uniform with golden buttons and a wide-brimmed hat, holding a sword or a long spyglass; sometimes he would have a wooden leg, or a scar, or a black patch over the eye ... and here comes this person that everyone calls captain. But much like this "kapitan," despite their appearance, all the other Israeli guys and ladies were also full of responsibility and motivation. And the responsibility was a heavy one to bear: to lead more than 4,000 people on one ship against the British army. Indeed, during the times of struggle and crisis and the obstacles that were yet to come, these young- sters proved their strength of spirit and resourcefulness. I didn't know much about their endeavors at the time –the adults told me about them later—but as a child I felt a deep sense of admiration towards them, and they made me feel a strong sense of confidence and hope when they were around.

The elated holiday spirit, which had already started to fade with the appearance of the British plane, changed quickly into one of suspense and stress when a small dot was noticed on the surface of the sea from afar. Many tried to ignore it, at first, as if it was a mirage or some annoying fly, but slowly the dot grew bigger and transformed into a gray and menacing battleship with the British flag hanging from its stern. The rumors started to pass from mouth to ear and questions were being asked: Where did the ship come from? What for? Many among us tried to relieve our worries with the thought that the battleship was just passing through, that it was on its way to nowhere and would soon leave us be. But the anxiety was ongoing and we knew that our hopes were in vain. The British ship approached us to a threatening proximity and then distanced itself a bit, sailing alongside the Exodus while keeping its distance but also the same rhythm. We went to sleep.

At dawn we saw more battleships; the following day there was another and each day more ships were added until a menacing dark fleet of seven British warships gathered around us. The ships drew closer and farther away intermittently. Loudspeakers sent demands of unconditional surrender towards our ship—"you have no chance of getting to shore," the messages said. There was no response from our ship; we were completely ignoring the Brits, at least on the outside. The radio in the center of the ship was calling for people not to get excited or panic, and melodies and marching songs were sounded to strengthen our spirits. Despite it all, the fears among the Ma'apilim grew stronger, and words like "war" and "battle" were repeated many times. On the sixth day, assemblies gathered on each deck to explain the situation. The emissaries from the Land of Israel announced very clearly that the British fleet was about to attack Exodus the next morning, when we entered the territorial waters of Israel. "The battle will be difficult," they said. "We should protect ourselves and prepare." Despite everything, we were told that the chances of breaking through and coming ashore were great, since we would be close to shore when the attack began. The ship would defend herself, and along the coast, from north to south, Palmach units and members of many settlements were ready to receive us as soon as the ship arrived. The battle was supposed to take place during the day, but the landing was planned to take place during the evening and night hours, in darkness. The residents were told that when the alarm sounded, they should close all the doors and windows that faced the balconies, leave the cabins, assemble at the center of the ship and sit as low as possible in order to avoid injuries from bullets or grenades.

During the early lunch hours, a frenzied activity took place inside the ship. Adults and children, mainly activists of the pioneer youth movements, started spreading metal nets and barbed-wire fences on the balconies and the decks, in order to prevent British soldiers from entering through these openings. Clubs, bottles, stones, glass and metal tools and anything that could be thrown or used as a weapon in battle were dispersed in many places along the decks. Many people among the Ma'apilim contributed personal equipment for the cause, such as kitchenware, knives, hammers and other tools. Everything was done quickly and in perfect order, while the Israeli guys ran from station to station, from deck to deck, working, improving, fixing, assembling nets and fences and throughout all that never forgetting to encourage us and give us a sense of confidence. Most of them were tired and exhausted, but it didn't show on their faces. Towards the evening, all the barricades and stations were set and the ship was ready for battle.

During this time, all kinds of people would appear trying to encourage us and give us a sense of confidence. A small group of three or maybe four guys, wearing dark blue shirts with azure stripes and many ornaments, made the most efforts in that area. They introduced themselves as members of the Beitar youth movement, and one of them made a long, enthusiastic and excited speech. This speech consisted of many words like "courage," "victory," "blood," "Jewish blood," "Jewish honor," "death," and many more. It was hard for me to understand his words, but one part of his speech left a strong impression on me and led me to thoughts that never stopped: in the midst of his speech, I slowly started to realize that he was bad-mouthing the Israeli guys. He mentioned the names Etzel and Lechi with respect and pride and scorned the Haganah and the Palmach. His words were hard for me, since first of all I didn't understand why when everybody else was working and barricading, these four guys were idling and giving speeches. But mostly, I couldn't understand why those who had won the admiration of all the kids should be bad-mouthed, while they were at that same time working hard to barricade the ship and prepare it for battle. Without noticing, I started comparing the sloppily clothed guys with the Zabar Hebrew, who were upfront, blunt and confident, to the guys with the fancy clothes, who spoke Yiddish with a hoity-toity speech but with an obvious lack of confidence. I remembered that vision well.

The kids in the second grade in the Tel Nordau Elementary School in the year 1948 were great connoisseurs of internal politics. *Arguments about Etzel, Lechi, Haganah, and Palmach became routine. I, of course, sided with the Haganah and the Palmach, with the images before the fight of the Exodus still fresh in my mind. I was part of the majority in those discussions; those who sided with the Etzel and Lechi were the minority. Among them, a chubby short kid, who passionately defended his stance, stood out;*

he would go on and on and wasn't afraid to stand against the majority. I wasn't friends with this boy, but his fight against the masses triggered my respect towards him. Occasionally during the debates he would talk about conquering Jaffa and the heroism of the Etzel and Lechi members in that fight. His words impressed me very much, for I knew about Jaffa and its dangers, since I was living on Hayarden Street, which turned towards the sea, extremely close to Hayarkon Street, which passed from Northern Tel Aviv all the way to Jaffa. The mere mention of the name of Hayarkon Street would spark a shudder through my spine, for on its southern end, on the border with Jaffa, was the Hasan Beck mosque, and from the tower of that mosque the Arabs would shoot along Hayarkon Street. Many people were injured as a result of the shooting and I was afraid when I was near that street. I always crossed it running. The multistoried buildings on Hayarden Street, like ours, were also threatened from the mosque and bullets hit the porch wall above our windows; obviously, we were not allowed to go on the porch. They tried to build up a protective wall along Hayarkon Street that would block the bullets, but its efficiency was limited, for the mosque tower was higher than the wall. Only after Jaffa was conquered by Etzel[7] and Lechi[8] did the quiet return to Hayarkon Street, but not for very long.

7   *The common Israeli name for Irgun Tzvai-Leumi, or Irgun, an organization operating in the British Mandate of Palestine from 1931 to 1948.*

8   *Lehi (Hebrew pronunciation: [leχi]; Hebrew: לח"י – לוחמי חרות ישראל Lohamei Herut Israel - Lehi, "Fighters for the Freedom of Israel - Lehi"), commonly referred to in English as the Stern Gang,[8] was a militant Zionist group founded by Avraham ("Yair") Stern in the British Mandate of Palestine.*

One morning, I saw armed men fanning along the streets that turn towards the beach, and on the beach itself, in front of Frishman Street where my school was situated, a big iron ship was anchored. The armed men divided into two rival camps: on the one side were soldiers in the newly established army, the Israeli Defense Forces *(IDF), which was mostly based on Haganah and Palmach[9] men; on the other side were Etzel members. The northern streets—from Gordon through Frishman and all the way to Trumpeldor—were under the control of the IDF; the southern streets, including Hayarden Street, were under the control of Etzel. The two camps stood one in front of the other with the barricades situated on both sides of Trumpeldor Street. There was a lot of tension in the entire area and it was dangerous to be on the streets. My situation was especially difficult for the street I lived in was under the control of Etzel, while my school was dominated by the IDF. I couldn't walk to school through the main streets, because the armed guards on both sides didn't allow it. I found a secret path in between fences and yards, and so I would cross another "border" on my way to school. While I was running to class, two strong explosions were heard. We all ran to the shelter, which was nothing but a corridor barricaded with a stone wall. After a time there was silence again. I came back home from school, the armed*

---

9   *The Palmach (Hebrew:*פלמ"ח*, acronym for Plugot Ma'atz (Hebrew:*פלוגות מחץ*), lit. "strike forces") was the elite fighting force of the Haganah, the underground army of the Yishuv (Jewish community) during the period of the British Mandate for Palestine.*

forces scattered, "the border" disappeared. The ship, whose name was Altalena, had been bombed and was leaning on its side. Many months later people were still diving and taking rusty guns and pistols out of the sea. What happened there, anyway? The arguments in class heated up, the worrier-child told us that Altalena was bombed under Ben Gurion's orders, that people were killed there and that the ship contained weapons for the young country. "It's not true," responded the others. "The weapons were for Etzel so it could take over the country," the warrior-child furiously rejected the claim. "Then why weren't the guns immediately handed to the army?" I asked. "They wanted to, but under certain conditions ..." responded the boy. The conditions were complicated, as was this entire affair. Once again I wasn't able distinguish between good and evil, and again there was no black and white. I felt perplexed.

After dark, the British battleships approached us, lit their spotlights and started transmitting their demands of unconditional surrender. These were answered with a volley of stones. The battleships receded and distanced themselves from us; they turned the spotlights and loudspeakers off and a quiet and tense night befell Exodus. According to all the explanations we received, the actual British attack was supposed to start at dawn, with our entry into the territorial waters of Israel. Yet we were ordered to remain alert and ready from the beginning of the night.

In the middle of the night we felt slight jerks and the general sensation that the ship suddenly increased its speed. The Israeli guys went from cabin to cabin and quietly ordered us to step off our bunks, close the doors and windows, turn the lights out and sit on the floor of the inner corridor of the ship, which continued racing forward at a speed we weren't accustomed to. The ship sailed quickly and we anxiously awaited what was next to come. Hours before the time we were told to expect an attack, a loud noise sounded and a great concussion stirred the entire ship. The ship and the balconies trembled and squeaked and it felt like it was going to break apart. Spotlights shone on the ship and their light penetrated through the cracks in the windows and doors into the inner corridor. Cries from the loudspeakers again demanded the commanders of the Exodus to surrender to avoid a catastrophe. Explosions and gunfire were heard, bumps and shocks were felt as the British ships knocked our ship. Teargas bombs penetrated the inner decks. My dad pulled out some handkerchiefs, wetted them with some water from the canteen and handed them to us. We put the handkerchiefs on our eyes and sat cramped up on the floor of the inner corridor.

The explosions, the noise and the shooting all reminded me of the night of our escape from Odessa. Is this what a war looks like? I asked myself how such a war would end. Would we live or die? Uncertainty reigned everywhere. The jerking grew more and more frequent, more teargas penetrated the ship, more shooting occurred. Suddenly we saw people covered in blood streaming towards the inner deck; some had every part of their bodies bandaged. Guys with stretchers were running to and fro with the more severely wounded. I removed the handkerchief from my eyes occasionally and once saw a tall, dark and muscular man running along the corridor, his face covered in blood, his shirt torn, a bandage covering half his face. He was running and shouting: "Fight! Fight! Never surrender!" Suddenly the lights inside the ship went out and the spotlight from outside disappeared. I fell to the side, and it felt as if the ship had suddenly stopped, turned around and started moving again in the opposite direction. I didn't understand the meaning of it and the silence afterwards was also weird. Only later did I find out that the ship had an extra engine and these resourceful guys turned it on, escaped the surrounding British ships and tried to return and sail towards the Israeli shore. We continued sailing like this for what seemed like an eternity, until a great thrust, stronger than anything that preceded it, frightened us all. People started screaming inside the ship, the sounds of gunfire and the explosions of teargas grenades returned along with the spotlight. Wounded people started running through the corridor again. We heard explosions and strong hammering sounds and suddenly soldiers with dark khaki uniforms, white helmets, and clubs in one hand and guns in the other broke through the inner door to the corridor. They were British soldiers. Some people in the corridor started shouting and attacking the soldiers, but they shook them off and mumbled something that sounded like an embarrassed apology in an incomprehensible language. A huge flood of soldiers in white helmets started moving along the corridor; screams sounded from other decks, but slowly the battle sounds subsided. A relative silence took over. The wounded continued to pass through the corridor, some of them on stretchers. Some were moaning, others were quiet. I saw a few of the guys with the forelocks. Their clothes were torn, some were wounded and stained with blood. They were dirty, with carbonized faces. There were also people who were led by the soldiers to who knows where.

"A ship scouts in secret" and now it was over. Nothing helped; neither the hope nor the heroism, nor the confidence nor the smile. None could survive in front of seven well-equipped battleships attacking a maladroit overburdened river ship. They attacked hours too soon, "against the law, in international waters," so we've been told. The British were afraid that this ship with so many passengers might make it to shore so they precipitated the attack. The Israeli guys didn't take that into account.

While my eyes were filled with tears due to the gas, and anxiety and despair was visible on everyone's faces, I felt the ship turning again, moving slowly forward with mild jerks, leaning to the right. The rocking of the ship made me fall asleep. I had a troubled sleep on the deck floor and bad dreams haunted me: trains, gunshots, cannons, white helmets, blood—it was all mixed in a great big confusion in my head. I woke in the morning and everything around me looked like a nightmare: wreckage, ruins, split walls, blood-covered bandages, people rotting, sleeping or staring at the ceiling, lying on the floor. Despair reigned everywhere: hopelessness, lack of purpose. There were no more songs sounding on the radio, the members of the youth movements didn't circle around with words of encouragement, there were no more guys with forelocks. A British soldier with a white helmet stood at the entrance. He was all clean and pressed, with a white belt hanging diagonally across his shirt. When the soldier saw me waking up, he approached me and offered me a piece of candy. I took the candy, aimed towards his face and threw it. The candy missed his face, hitting the helmet and making a ringing sound. The soldier reproached me with his index finger, said a few words, laughed and went away.

I opened the door of our cabin and walked quietly inside. Outside it was light already; I opened the outer door and went out onto the balcony. Here and there people stood along the decks in small groups. I saw torn iron nets ripped to pieces, broken banisters, and remnants of bottles, stones and other weapons scattered on the floors. British soldiers walked around the decks. An elderly couple stood on the balcony, near our cabin—a religious, bearded man and a short fat woman. They stood there facing the sea and crying. When they saw me they pulled me towards the banister, held me between them, turned my face forward and shouted into my ear: "Look child! The Land of Israel!" and burst into tears again. Their cries were filled with longing and hope, but also held disappointment and depression. With this cry they were telling me: "Child, look, here is the land we wanted so much to come to and now we can't even touch it."

I looked out; it was a hot and steamy summer day. Vapor rose from the sea and a thin mist covered the coastline, which was full of ships and boats of all shapes and sizes. I looked up and saw a mountain, with a forest sliding down the slippery slope into the sea, and inside the forest were small white houses. This image was so magical, so peaceful, so much in contrast to the horrific visions of the previous night. I felt like it was a wonderland, a land of dreams, and I wanted to fly from the ship towards the sylvan mountain. I was looking at that sight, which was Haifa, the slope of the Carmel Mount descending towards the sea. It was my first image of the land of dreams. If someone asks me what Israel is to me, and I answer "everything," it might be the truth, but not the entire truth, for my personal image of the Land of Israel was that of the woody Carmel Mount descending into the beach, with the white houses and the misty coastline.

The year was 1956. *I went to the ministry of internal affairs to receive my identity card. Filling out the questionnaire, I wrote: country of birth—Israel; city of birth—Haifa. What's the problem, I asked myself, was this the first time I had a fake ID card?! Two weeks later I received my card and opened it with a nervous tremble, but my hands fell with disappointment. The card was indifferent to my emotional turmoil and on it was written in black ink on white paper: country of birth—Soviet Union; city of birth—Stalinabad. I guess ID cards can't always be forged, and Stalinabad was false, anyhow.*

But I didn't give up. I hid the card and proudly told my friends at work, at the national print office in Tel Aviv, that I was from Haifa. Was it a complete lie?! Of course not, for it was in Haifa, in front of the Carmel, that I was reborn.

I shook off the exciting sight and looked to the foot of the mountain. I saw the harbor and the streets, when suddenly I heard shouts from the streets. A multitude of people filled the port gate, carrying signs, shouting slogans, waving their hands. The citizens of Haifa had come out for a protest of solidarity with the Ma'apilim from the Exodus. A tough and rude British soldier passed along the deck and made us go inside to our cabins. I went back to my cabin in silence with thoughts running through my head. My parents were busy again, for the millionth time, with packing our meager belongings for the next chapter of nomadism.

Chapter Eight

"The Hope of Two Thousand Years"

As we were packing our belongings, a Haganah member came to our cabin and described to us the progress of the nightly battle: the Brits attacked in international waters, against the law, for otherwise we would come ashore. He told us that the ship had an extra engine that was turned on to accelerate our speed, fearing that the Brits would indeed attack prematurely. We were correct in feeling the ship accelerating. He confirmed another feeling we had—that of the ship turning backwards—and recounted the trick that almost worked, which was performed with the help of the extra engine in the stern. Indeed, we felt the ship escaping the surrounding battleships, and that it was coming closer to shore. But destiny changed that move: a powerful, unintended clash in the dark with a British battleship. That was the clash that shook the entire vessel.

As a result, an entire wall fell in the center of the ship, a number of people fell to sea and drowned, many others were injured and the ship began to sink. In such a situation, there was no choice but to surrender, to avoid the sinking of the ship and us all being killed. The Brits tied the ship to one of their battleships and towed it to the military port in Haifa.

We were also told about the protests of solidarity in Israel and the entire world for the sake of the Ma'apilim. I witnessed some of the demonstrations with my own eyes at the port gate in Haifa. He also solemnly promised that the Haganah would not rest until every one of the Ma'apilim on the Exodus arrived to Israel as quickly as possible. "But in the meantime," he said sadly, "the Brits will transfer you to floating cages—three deportation ships—that will take you to the detention camps in Cyprus, which is a two-day sailing distance from Israel. That is the procedure against what they call illegal immigration," he said. The last words of the Haganah member were encouraging; amidst all the despair and depression there was a shred of hope, for despite what happened, Cyprus was still close to the Israeli shores and it would be easy to escape from there and reach the long-awaited beaches of Israel. Hope—false as it may be—has a great deal of charm that bestows strength to the people in their continuation of suffering. If only he knew, if only we had known, what was ahead of us, the truth, who knows what would have happened. We might have fought, or perhaps refused to board the floating cages. The military organizations might have tried to perform some kind of bold rescue operation ... but no! We couldn't have guessed what was about to happen, and this time, the Brits tricked us and the Israeli guys once again. He left and we finished our packing.

A large group of British soldiers with red caps boarded the ship. They were the paratroopers from the British garrison in Israel; the adults called them "Anemones." They treated us far differently than the soldiers with the white helmets. Those with the helmets were seamen on the battleships and they treated us with kindness and tolerance. They apologized to English-speaking immigrants dozens of times for the job they were given; they told them that they didn't want to obey the orders and that they did it out of a sense of duty to the orders they were given. The "Anemones," on the other hand, were snobbish, and at times even hostile and violent. They pushed the people towards the decks and the gangplank that led from the ship down to the pier in the harbor. We descended to the rugged cement pier under armed guards, and I saw the wounded descending too. Everyone pointed at one of the wounded with admiration, saying: "There is Mordechai, who bravely fought the British last night." Overnight, he went from being a John Doe, a youth instructor in HaShomer Hatzair, to an admired hero, the unofficial leader of the Ma'apilim. He became the confidant of the Israeli guys throughout the entire Via Dolorosa we were about to undergo. His orders were fulfilled quickly and his authority among the Ma'apilim was natural and obvious.

The human queue resumed much like the one during our boarding in the French harbor, but how different it was. No more singing, no elevated spirits—only tension and anxiety for what was to come, a never-ending swing between hope and despair. When I reached the pier, I looked backwards and saw the giant hole in the ship wall, right underneath the name Exodus. Again, I saw the decks with the torn-down nets, ropes dangling from the decks, "Anemones" walking back and forth. The ship stood silent, a bit tilted—a giant monster, a sort of a legendary Minotaur that died a long time ago.

July 1985. *Very hot weather. Thirty-seven years have passed since we left the Exodus. It is no longer seen from the Carmel slope. The ship has been gone for many years; it was dismantled and its remains buried at sea. The harbor developed and there was no room for such junk anymore, even if it was loaded with memories and history. Only a small model remained at the museum by the sea, near the cave of the prophet Eliyahu. I went in search of the remnants of the past and entered the clandestine immigration museum that is found inside a small ship that remained intact, called "Af Al Pi Chen" (translation from Hebrew: "And despite it all"). The Exodus model stands close to the entrance, a small* *and beautiful toy, polished; postcards with the picture of the model were on sale. But I didn't want to buy them; I didn't feel anything towards that model—that wasn't the real Exodus. The real one came to life for a little while, when an audio-visual film about the history of clandestine immigration was shown. On screen I saw the Exodus alive and breathing with its black chimney, Mordechai fighting the Brits, the "Anemones," the seamen with the white helmets, the open hole in the wall, the torn protection nets. But the specatcle was over and nothing remained save the toy at the entrance.*

We were walking on the pier surrounded by British soldiers pushing us to go forward. Across the fence, Haifa residents were shouting, waving their hands, trying to cheer us. The feeling of frustration was deep and profound; it was but mere unluckiness that we were here, on this side of the fence instead of there, on that other side, protesting freely. I dreamed for a moment that none of it had ever happened, that we were disembarking calmly from the ship on our way to the gate, to freedom, to Haifa, passing the gate and climbing the Carmel slope. But the dream didn't last for long. Two British female soldiers with a red cross on their sleeves grabbed me hard and one of them sprayed me with a white powder using a hand sprayer; everyone received that kind of treatment. "Against lice," we were told. And while we were still stunned by the humiliating spectacle, we were pushed towards a long table. Sitting at the table were Brits, some in uniform and some in civilian clothes, asking the grown-ups about their identities: "What is your name?" "Where did you come from?" To my surprise, no one answered with coherent answers, including my parents. They all answered the same thing: "I am a Jew from the Land of Israel." This was an order made by Haganah that was circulated among the clandestine immigrants and carried out by everyone. Any attempts the Brits made to convince the people to give out real details failed miserably. No one had any documents and so the tiresome and monotonous journey along the table lasted for many hours. In the meantime, the passengers' belongings were carefully examined and the British removed and confiscated objects such as knives, can openers, nails, atlases, magnets, compasses, and the like. The removal of the compasses had a special meaning that would be revealed later.

It was almost evening when we were led towards the three ships that stood tied to faraway piers. The ships looked like giant iron cages, with a big belly and a little deck on top of which stood the command and steering pavilion and the quarters of the staff and soldiers. Above the deck were chimneys. Those were extremely ugly-looking ships, especially compared to the Exodus, which had a special charm. We started going up the gangplank into one of the floating cages—the larger among the three. *Empire Rival* was written on the iron frame; this was the name of the deportation ship—the floating cage in which we were about to float during the next period. We descended into the belly of the ship. The crowding there was hard to bear and our spirits were also down. With this kind of background and the hard conditions we had to deal with, it was only natural that there would be friction between people with different behaviors and characters. The quarrels were hard and incessant; we had a fight with a big, fat, bald man. He was a widower who was staying next to us, and for some reason he and my parents didn't see eye to eye. Each family grabbed a piece of the ship's iron floor, spreading blankets over it; everyone lived together in one big hall. The guys and girls from Haganah went underground, and so they wouldn't be recognized by the British they changed their identities; they no longer wore shorts and sandals but wore clothes like ours. Yet we still recognized them and their authority was as great as before. Two of them were on our ship, a man and a woman. The man was nicknamed "Gad" and the woman "Sima." Their presence encouraged us and gave us hope. Together with the people from Haganah two other groups were hiding among us as well: American volunteers and Moroccan volunteers, graduates of the pioneer youth movements. The Brits were feverishly looking for members of these two groups and they needed to be hidden.

As we were settling in our corner on the iron floor, Gad and Sima appeared with a thin dark-skinned fellow. They spoke quietly with my parents and at the end of the conversation he joined our family as a rightful member, a "cousin."

I was told quietly that he was a volunteer from Morocco who was working as a seaman on the Exodus alongside the guys from Israel and the United States. He didn't know Hebrew or Yiddish or any other language we spoke, only French and Arabic, and we had to use hand gestures to communicate. Despite the language difficulties we became good friends. He used to make funny charades and faces that made me and my sister laugh. The guy was a young sloppy bachelor and my mom used to mend clothes and socks for him while he tried unsuccessfully to teach us some French. One day, we discovered that we—or rather Mom, to be more accurate—had a common language with him. He started singing a song and Mom was moved because she understood a phrase in it, which was in the Ladino language. Many years ago, in Russia, Mom was a kindergarten teacher for orphan children from the Spanish civil war. She could speak Spanish and Ladino is an ancient Spanish language, so the Moroccan guy started speaking Ladino and Spanish with my mom.

The situation in the belly of the ship was unbearable. A small ladder led from the deck down to where the iron walls were burning from the heat. People were sweating and suffocating as a result of the heat; the congestion was horrible and there were no windows in the big cage hall, only two barred openings over the ceiling. The suffocating atmosphere led people to climb the ladder hoping to get some fresh air, but the British soldiers limited that option.

Everyone shared the ship floor in such a way that the youth movements and the orphan houses were in one section, while the families and singles were in another, but in fact, there was no difference and we all lived together in one big stuffy, hot hall.

When it was dark we began feeling small jerks; it was obvious that the ship had set sail. I fell asleep with the hope that the suffering inside the cage would be short and that tomorrow afternoon, or evening at the latest, we would get to Cyprus. We would stay in a camp there, which I imagined to be similar to the one in Ainring, Germany.

When I woke up in the morning, the heat was heavy. They gave us a pack of dry biscuits in a tin box with some turbid tea. This was "breakfast," and the meals that came afterwards were the same. Stale soup or potatoes were added at times, but that was it.

I climbed the ladder onto the deck. The bars were open and being there made me feel good. The sea breeze was blowing despite the heat, and the suffocating atmosphere from the belly of the ship was gone. Topless British soldiers were playing ping pong, laughing and shouting. Some of them approached us and handed us candies. Their good mood was also related to the supposed fact that we were finally arriving at Cyprus, and then they would be rid of us and the burden of leading thousands of refugees there in

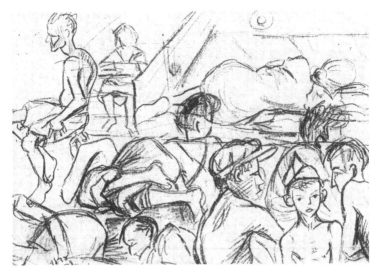

In the belly of the "Empire Rival" deportation ship.
Painting by Ada Benisho, a clandestine immigrant from France

prison ships. Neither the soldiers, nor the guards, nor we, the prisoners, had any idea about the real destination of the floating cages. I took the candy and this time I didn't throw it at the soldier but gladly sucked on it. It tasted great compared to the dry biscuits. I looked around but saw nothing but sea. Every now and then I would imagine seeing a shore and thought it was Cyprus, but it was all an illusion; there was nothing but the calm, blue, hot sea, smooth as a mirror.

I came back down to the cage and the suffocating heat. There was nothing to do; boredom, nervousness and idleness reigned everywhere, but everyone drew strength from the fact that in a few hours we would be in Cyprus. It was nighttime, with no shore in sight. I went to sleep feeling nervous. Dreams of trains and gunshots returned to haunt me. When I woke in the morning, the adults were extremely edgy. Well-hidden compasses that had been smuggled aboard appeared from nowhere and revealed the truth: the ship was not sailing north to Cyprus, but west. I went up to the deck and saw the two other cages sailing in the same direction. The British soldiers who were on deck were also perplexed and nervous and didn't know the meaning of this. Horrifying rumors about sailing to Africa, Mauritius, Australia and God-knows-where were circulating among the immigrants. The rage in the cage was overwhelming; many people tried to break onto the deck, and in response the Brits closed the openings and rolled barbed-wire fences on top of them. The exit to the deck was temporarily prohibited.

The grown-ups were filled with rage: "The Brits conned us again. If we had known the destination was not Cyprus, events would not have passed so quietly in Haifa, a war would have broken out, and we would have opposed boarding the deportation ships by force." No one knew exactly what the final destination of the deportation ships was. No one understood why the route changed and no one could predict how horrible the end of the journey would be. Sima and Gad had no answers or explanations; their attempts to get information from the British soldiers failed, but they promised that they would try to contact the Haganah headquarters soon to try to figure out the meaning of the westward sailing direction.

In the meantime, another day and night passed. The biscuits were becoming moldy, there were worms in all the tin cans, the food became scarcer and there had been no fruits or vegetables since we set sail. Diseases started spreading among the stealthy immigrants. The deck could only be boarded for a little while, and attempts to lift the bars by force were made but were stopped by the British soldiers. The heat led most people to strip down to their undergarments, natural embarrassment fading under such conditions. At night, the feet of the British guards would knock on the iron floor and we would recognize the guards who were going to and fro at a nerve-wracking pace.

On one of the days, a rumor circulated among the ship's residents that we passed the shores of Italy and were heading towards France. Haganah members communicated to us news that the Brits were planning to take us to France, to the harbor from which Exodus had sailed, and make us leave the ship by force. The news was hard and shocking. The Brits had never done anything like that before; they would always deport illegal immigrants that were caught to Cyprus and here we were experiencing a change in policy. The adults assumed they were doing it to "teach the Jews a lesson," once and for all. As punishment for daring to sail such a big ship with so many people to the

A typical image of the residents of the "Empire Rival."
Painting by Ada Benisho, an illegal immigrant from France.

coast of Israel, they had decided to take it back to Europe, to its port of departure, hoping that such a move would "end the illegal immigration." Gad and Sima promised that Haganah would not abandon the clandestine immigrants of Exodus and its members would reach any place the deportation ships may anchor; but there was little comfort in those words. The tension increased the friction between the clandestine immigrants and the British soldiers. They became more tough and edgy, and the clashes led to additional limitations on time spent on the decks, as well as rationing of the food portions.

I felt my gums beginning to swell. My temperature rose and the doctor who examined me ordered me transferred to a hospital that was located in a different section of the ship. They lay me on a bed, and I had fever-generated delusions. I developed scurvy, a disease caused by the lack of fruits and vegetables. It was common among seamen of previous generations and disappeared after Captain Cook, one of Britain's most estimated seamen, successfully fought it with sauerkraut. Therefore it was ironic that on a British ship, in the twentieth century, it would resurface. The disease caught me during a very delicate stage when my permanent teeth were in the process of coming in, and as a result I had bad teeth for the rest of my life.

While I was lying in the hospital, delirious, bleeding, having nightmares, screaming from the heat and shaking to and fro on the hard cot, the prison ships were approaching the coast of France. Again a hectic political campaign was held over our heads, much like before the sailing of the Exodus: intrigues, press conferences, declarations, and rallies across the world for the clandestine immigrants and against Britain, petitions and protests.

In the heavy heat, while we were all sweating and nervous, and people were lying feverish in the hospital, the three ships arrived at the coast of France and anchored in a small port called *Porte de Buc*, not far from the harbor where we boarded the Exodus on our way to Israel. In such a short time our fortune had changed: we left the French coast in high spirits, free, proud and full of hope for a new life, and here we were, returning to the same coast hungry and thirsty, feverish, wearing ragged clothes and imprisoned. There was uncertainty in the air, threats and dangers. How can the people stand any more suffering? How can they stand the constant reduction in living conditions, which was established by the British as a means to pressure the clandestine immigrants?

While the ships were anchored in front of the coast, but at a large distance, powerful loudspeakers were turned on in the cages and messages in several languages were communicated to the Ma'apilim, saying: "His Majesty's government hereby announces to the illegal passengers that for humanitarian purposes it will allow them to leave the deportation ships and disembark safely to the French shore, from which they sailed not long ago." The messages were repeated and provoked angry responses even in the hospital. One of the messages included threats and said that if people did not leave willfully, the Brits would use force. Cries were heard throughout the hospital, nurses and doctors ran inside trying to calm the patients, but to no avail.

The ship suffered through one or two days of tension and then suddenly there were fruits and vegetables in the hospital. Eating them sped up my recovery and in a few days I left the hospital and was back in the big hall in jail. Out of all the produce I was offered, I especially remember the little red tomatoes from the fields of Provence; those were the best-tasting tomatoes I have ever eaten. I also remember the watermelons. In addition to the food, we started to receive books, notebooks, pencils and even games. There were checkers, chess, dominoes and picture cards, but I loved the different puzzles most of all. While I was in the hospital, they brought me a puzzle I worked on day and night. It had a picture of a forest, a wolf and a house; it might have been the story of Little Red Riding Hood or Peter and the Wolf.

During that time, in the middle of the transfer of the supplies, different events took place inside the ships and around them. Distinguished delegations would come to visit the cages; among them were French generals with elliptic hats. The delegations would use a ladder to descend into the cages, but once the sight was revealed to them and the horrible smells of urine and sweat hit them, they recoiled, stopped and retreated.

When we would go up to the deck, we could see little boats circling around the ship, approaching and sounding encouraging cries for the Ma'apilim. These cries and the messages were a source of power that strengthened the spirit of the people, their stamina and their determined decision not to descend to the French shores but demand to be taken back to the Land of Israel. At times there were also cries stating the support of the French people to the Ma'apilim. A boat with a red flag approached and cheered in the name of the French unions. Boats with delegates from Haganah would approach and transfer coded messages to the Haganah members inside the ships. The British tried to disrupt this by distancing the ships from one another, but nothing helped. Once, in order to transfer a message from our ship to another deportation ship, one of the people jumped from the deck into the sea and started swimming fast towards the other ship, but the Brits sent a boat, pulled him out of the water and brought him back to our ship. The fresh supply of food kept on coming, which was at least some compensation for the stress and uncertainty.

La HAGANA s'adresse aux réfugiés de l' "Exodus"

Au premier plan, un délégué de la Hagana sur une vedette munie d'un haut-parleur, adresse des exhortations aux réfugiés de l' « Exodus » qui se trouvent à bord d'un des « Liberty Ships » en rade de Port-de-Bouc.

Haganah boats transferring messages to one of the deportation ships
(from the collection of French news clips of Shmuel Lutzki, a
mathematician and engineer from Paris)

One day, we woke to turmoil. Gad and Sima were running around, transferring messages and preparing the Ma'apilim towards an extremely important event that was about to take place. The British guards on deck were also tense and nervous, feelings that could be heard through the knocking of shoes on our ceiling. Going up to the deck was prohibited. Around 10 a.m., the deck hatch opened and let in a large delegation of important men, wearing suits or army uniforms, ties, and some even hats. The heavy heat and the stench shocked them, they stopped, wiped their sweat and waved their handkerchiefs to ease the heat. They got used to the situation and then one of the leaders of the

Ma'apilim announced that a delegation from the French government had arrived to give the people an important message.

The head of the French delegation read a long speech, which was occasionally translated into Yiddish by one of the Ma'apilim. What I could grasp as a child I completed later with an explanation my parents gave me: the French government was sympathetic to the suffering of the Ma'apilim and condemned the British deportation policy. Yet, for humanitarian purposes, the French government offered refuge to any clandestine immigrant who wished it. Any single man or woman or a family who came ashore would have citizenship, proper housing, basic supplies, living expenses for the adaptation period and income sources. The French government prohibited the British from taking people off the ship by force. Furthermore, the aid with food, medicine and any other needed supplies would continue as long as the ships were anchored on the French coast. The French government also demanded that Britain find a quick solution to the suffering of the refugees if they did not accept the French offer.

The answer that was given by one of the leaders began with thanking the French government and the French people for their humane treatment and generous offer. But the offer was denied: "France is a beautiful, tolerant and humane country," he said, "but we are not French; this is not our motherland; we cannot return to European soil for we have a different destination—the Land of Israel." The speaker also addressed the French government, asking it to put pressure on Britain so they might set sail back to Israel and let the Ma'apilim descend there. "We will not leave the ship of our own free will to any shore that is not the Israeli coast," he said. Loud applause accompanied his last words, and then, spontaneously, we all rose to our feet as one person, and the members of the youth movements were the first to burst out singing:

As long as in the heart within,
A Jewish soul still yearns...

Everyone joined, those who knew the words and those that didn't, children, elderly, adults, whispering and aloud, and the singing became a loud and thundering cry:

Our hope is not yet lost,
The hope of two thousand years,
To be a free people in our land,
The land of Zion and Jerusalem.

The Israeli National Anthem, "Hatikvah"
Lyrics: Naftali Herz Imber

There were people crying during the song; a strong emotion took hold of the French delegation and some of its members started crying as well. It lasted a while, the Ma'apilim and members of the delegation remained standing silently. Slowly, people returned to sit on the floor and the delegation members came back to the deck and were gone. What impression did it leave on the French? It must have been grand! But I too received a special inspiration: I felt power, a sense of belonging and hope. I heard the "Hatikvah" for the first time in Ainring camp in Germany, but only now I could feel the great electrifying power this simple song possessed.

After the delegation left the ship and the Brits found out the result, there was a considerable worsening of their treatment towards us. They started creating difficulties with respect to food supplies from the shore and going up to the deck was prohibited. Tension reigned in the jail hall. Then a message came through the loudspeakers, which was one of the hardest and most bitter moments in the entire journey of the Exodus. The message stated: "Since the illegal passengers refused the kind offers made by France and Britain, and since the authorities cannot leave the ships at sea without any time limit, with no remaining alternative, His Majesty's government has decided to lead these people back to Germany and leave them there, in the occupied British zone. The passengers of the deportation ships still have time to repent and descend on the French coast." This extension lasted for a couple of days, if my memory serves me right.

The shock was horrible. The meaning of the bitter message did not sink in right away. Germany—the cursed and condemned land from which we were all running and never wanted to return, with so many of the Ma'apilim in death camps during the war, with so many losing their loved ones because of Germany—going back there was unthinkable. The people refused to believe it; they ran to Gad and Sima asking, "Could it be?!" but they didn't have any answers. Suddenly a small boat appeared in the sea and a message from the Haganah was heard from its loudspeakers. The message confirmed the bitter news, but the voice called the people to hold on, to remain strong, not to descend to the French coast and to fight against any attempt to make them leave the ship at the German shore. Haganah repeated its promise to accompany the ships to the German coast, take diplomatic measures with the other nations, but mostly the spokesman promised that the Haganah would never abandon the members of the Exodus, whatever happened. "You will be the first we bring to Israel," he said. This promise was indeed fulfilled.

The news was indeed bitter, but despite the blow, the people were filled with the willpower to refuse to descend to the French coast. Many still believed in secret that the British were only making threats and they wouldn't dare to carry out such an atrocity, not because they couldn't, but because the free world wouldn't allow them to do so. It was amazing how naïve those people who experienced every possible atrocity were.

A deep depression and anxiety spread throughout the cage at night. People were tense and exhausted. They quickly fell asleep and only the knocking of the shoes of the British guards could be heard from above. There was sleep, but it wasn't peaceful; people twisted from side to side, mumbling and dreaming. I had a nightmare too: "Anemones," dark forests, gun shots... suddenly, demons with white sheets and twisted faces were attacking me and making horrific cries. While I was half asleep and half awake, I continued hearing the cries and felt that I joined them and was crying with the demons too. I woke up, but I couldn't stop shouting, despite my will—I was shouting harder and a terrible and horrifying cry was rising around me. The lights in the jail hall lit up and then I saw myself and the rest of the people around me. Some were lying on the blankets, or sitting, heads turned upward, mouths open and yelling Aaaa... Aaaa... Terrified British soldiers were running around on the deck, the bars were opened, and armed guards were beginning to come down, turning flashlights and spotlights on, trying to figure out what was going on, but to no avail. Little by little, the cries subsided, the people calmed down, sat on the blankets, waking up from the collective nightmare and asking each other, "What happened?!" but no one knew the answer. I asked myself, too—why was I shouting? How was it that my private dream and my private cry was shared by everyone?! Later my parents tried to explain that someone started shouting because of a bad dream, and the others joined in in their sleep and the cries easily passed between the tired and nervous people and thus everyone was shouting at once— the pain, the frustration, the rage and the depression they felt manifested itself in one big desperate cry. I couldn't go back to sleep, and lay awake till the morning; the lights remained lit as well.

When the morning came, the engines were turned on and the ship began to shake in light jerks. The last remaining boats with loudspeakers still circled us cheering. The ship turned its bow towards the open sea and the three floating cages turned southwest, towards the Strait of Gibraltar.

Chapter Nine

"We Land and Sing"

Two grueling days passed until we saw a shore, a narrow shore that was confined by a cliff that descended steeply into the sea—the Rock of Gibraltar. The ships entered the British army port; the "Anemones" descended at the harbor for a two-day vacation and were replaced by soldiers with khaki caps. At first we were happy about the change, for we were tired of the "Anemones," with their intolerant and abrupt behavior, and they were probably sick of us too, with our problems. But our disappointment was deep, as the Gibraltar soldiers were much ruder and tougher than the "Anemones." There were violent clashes between us, and one of their first actions was to limit the area on the deck where we were allowed to walk and get some fresh air. The hatred towards these soldiers was so great that ironically we anxiously waited for the "Anemones" to come back, and they did, but we gained nothing from it. With the passing days, the relationship between us worsened, the attitude of the "Anemones" became tougher and the resistance from the Ma'apilim grew. Provocation and teasing on both parts became routine. All of us, the Ma'apilim and the "Anemones," were trapped inside this boiling steamer that was threatening to blow up any moment.

After two days anchored at port, we set sail and passed the strait of Gibraltar with the steep rock being clear and close to us, while far in the mist on the southern side a hazy image of the African coast could be seen. It was still hot, even after the ship had crossed the strait and entered the Atlantic Ocean. Several times during the maritime journey I thought about the meaning of the names of the different seas we passed through; I saw we were floating on the same water but first it was called the Mediterranean Sea, then Tyhhrenian Sea, Ligurian Sea, and so on. The waves remained the same, and the sun shone on them the same way. I asked my parents about this, and they explained with drawing maps on a paper with a crude pencil, geography, and historic reasons. Despite this I didn't understand, and so I waited impatiently for the passing—which this time seemed to be drastic—from the Mediterranean Sea into the Atlantic Ocean; besides, I wanted to see what an "ocean" was and what the difference between an "ocean" and a "sea" was. We passed the strait and nothing changed; everything remained the same. I was disappointed, thinking that the grown-ups were just making up names with no good reason. But pretty soon I realized my mistake and understood that there was a difference, after all.

The next morning, I came up on the deck again; everything seemed to be normal, until, suddenly, without any notice, the ship began to shake violently. I looked at the sea and saw huge waves running around the ship; their height was so scary I ran downstairs to the cage—it was the first time that I had seen such enormous waves. I decided not to succumb to fear and boarded the deck once again. The skies had become dark in the meantime, black heavy clouds were passing by quickly on their way to the east and the sea stormed with fury. The shattering waves sprinkled salty drops all over and some of them hit my face, stinging as they did so. The ship shook harder and harder, and I became nauseated and was sure that I was sick again and would be returned to the hospital. Soldiers dressed in capes appeared on the deck and urged me and all those that remained there to hurry and return downstairs to the cage. I came back to the cage, the ship continued to shake, and people were vomiting all around. I was told this was "seasickness" that appears when there is a storm and passes when the sea calms down. Despite all that was happening around me, my illness passed before the storm subsided, and I was proud of myself that I managed to hold on and overcome the "seasickness" on my own. During the storm I reached the conclusion that there was a difference between "sea" and "ocean" and my conclusion was clear and simple, even if not very scientific and certainly untrue: in my opinion, a "sea" was quiet waters, pleasant waves, no storms, no torments and constant heat. An "ocean," even if quiet for a short while, was usually stormy and cold.

There was no winter like the winter of .1951 *Storms, rain ,cold and even snow !Snow in Tel Aviv !?Who has ever seen or heard of such a thing ?Even the old folks in Tel Aviv didn't remember such a sight .The snow was soft and pleasant ,but outside it was freezing cold ,the skies were dark and the maritime horizon in the west was somber .I saw giant waves attacking the beach and the boardwalk from afar .I came down from the house and walked towards the boardwalk on the beach ;I came closer and saw a terrible sight .Huge waves were flooding the boardwalk and white froth was shattering and spraying all over the place .On top of the waves ,floating like carried-away leaves ,were boxes, timber ,floats ,automatic game machines and whatnot, anything the mind could think of .I stood there ,at some distance ,watching this grand spectacle both amazed and frightened ,and then I returned home .After a few days the storm subsided ,the weather improved and I returned to the beach to see and observe the results of the storm .The sight was one of total chaos .The boardwalk suffered a severe blow—benches and fences were torn down ;stacks of garbage that were ejected from the sea rested in disorder on the road ,on the sidewalks and at the entrances to buildings .I looked under the boardwalk ledge onto the sand on the coastline ,where huge shacks called Tir used to stand; inside them were game machines, slots, cafes and pool tables. I took a second look down and couldn't believe* *my eyes—the beach was smooth and clean with no remains of the big Tir. I realized that my "scientific" conclusions from several years before had no solid base. That spectacle made me understand the true force of the "sea" and that there was no difference in fact between that and the "ocean."*

During our sailing northward, our boredom and idleness grew, for children and adults alike. Anxiety and stress gave way to numbness and carelessness. The leaders and the people in charge saw it as deterioration and feared it, and then an idea was proposed to keep the children busy with studies. But they were not just any ordinary studies, but an original form of study, which was both interesting and symbolic. We received notebooks and pencils and were told to go to the deck. Once there, we were organized in four standing columns and ordered to lay our notebooks on the back of the person standing in front of us. The "teacher" then dictated to us different segments in Hebrew and we stood and wrote. Day in and day out, with a sense of sacred duty, we would go up to the deck and study in this fashion. The kid on whose back my notebook lay kept moving all the time, it was hard to concentrate and grasp what was being taught, but the feeling was divine. It was a blunt opposition in front of the amazed "Anemones." Our standing there had something special, something powerful, which could not be explained with words. There we were, standing in front of the people who had robbed us of our freedom, who limited our steps, who did not allow us to descend to the magical shore of Haifa, who tried to break us and make us get off the ship in France and were now leading us to the wretched Germany. And they stood there without understanding, unable to understand the human spirit that was unfolding before them in the form of little children, barefoot and ragged, standing on the deck of the floating cage each morning between the barbed-wire fences and studying like no one has ever studied before and no one will probably ever study again. This was repeated for several more days, and it was one of the highlights of our voyage.

The rumors about our coming near the German shores increased as did the tension over what was to come. The name of "Mordechai" from HaShomer HaTzair was mentioned again among the Ma'apilim. He was on another ship, but his orders were transmitted so that they reached us too; these specifically stated: it was our obligation to oppose the attempts of the British soldiers to take people off the ship at the German coast, by force, if necessary. There was great anxiety on the ship, for our ship contained the biggest concentration of children, elderly people and pregnant women. We feared that there might be casualties during our coming ashore.

The ship entered a big gulf, which was the Elbe Estuary to the North Sea. At the beginning, the gulf was wide with little islands and many ships that sailed to and fro. Little by little the gulf closed and became a river or a canal. We were

approaching the city of Hamburg, and Hamburg was controlled by the British. There were piers, with ships, trains,
trucks and a whole lot of noise, on both sides of the canal.
Port workers and seamen were standing there, loading and
unloading merchandise, with many cranes in the background. Our ship passed by a ship with an American flag
waving from its stern. Groups of black seamen were gathered around the ship and on it. When we passed it, the
American ship started honking hard and the black seamen
started waving their hands, making the "V" sign with their
fingers and pointing towards the opposite direction, that
is, towards the Land of Israel. The American seamen knew
where we were headed and what our biggest wish was, and
in a humane gesture they wished us to accomplish that. It
was a gesture of a people who had suffered towards another
people who were familiar with suffering. When they saw the
"Anemones," the black seamen started to direct clenched
fists at them and to curse them. Among the curses I heard
the phrase "Bevin-Hitler," which was sounded often by the
Ma'apilim towards the British soldiers during the fight on
the Exodus as well as afterwards. It turned out that the
comparison between the British foreign minister who was
perceived as being responsible for our suffering and Hitler
had passed from the Ma'apilim onwards and even reached
the ears of black seamen from the United States who had
no part in the affair.

The ships were approaching the pier; our belongings
were packed despite the intention to resist the descent

by force. Activists from the youth movements returned to circle around us, cheering us again, but this time with tears in their eyes. But then came the command that the clandestine immigrants on the deportation ship Empire Rival to not oppose by force but descend quietly, for that ship contained the biggest number of those that were not fit for battle: children, elderly and pregnant women. A deep disappointment spread on the faces of the cadets of the youth movements, but most of the people received the order without protest, for it was a humane command that took into account the concern for the lives of the people. With time, we learned that instead of a violent opposition, it was decided to teach the British a lesson in a different way—by blowing up the ship after the Ma'apilim descended. The bomb with the delay mechanism was planted by the painter Ada Benisho before she went to shore. The Brits found the bomb in time and managed to neutralize it.

With pent-up rage we started to descend from the deck when a view that enraged the Ma'apilim was revealed: Hamburg Port was completely full; masses of Germans had come to witness the descent, and the clandestine immigrants interpreted it as gloating and the wish to see once again how Jews were being abused on their cursed land. The Germans in the port were sitting on windows, balconies, rooftops of different buildings and even the rooftops of the train carts that were standing near the piers. Many

German police officers mixed with members of the British army and the military police were circling around. In the presence of that sight, the people's endurance failed and with clenched fists they started shouting and cursing at the Germans and the Brits, but they only responded with laughter and the humiliation was hard to bare. A terrible danger of a violent struggle was in the air; the command to resist opposition was about to lose its validity and the leaders worked hard to calm everyone down. "Hatikvah" sounded once more from somewhere. The hope in the words of the song and the actual singing managed to dissipate some of the tension and the Germans, along with the Brits, became silent in the presence of such a demonstration of the power of the spirit and the soul. Little by little we began to descend the gangplank to the pier. From afar there were train carts with bars on the windows, to which the British soldiers were leading us. From a distance, from the two other deportation ships, great cries could be heard and a large contingent of British soldiers took their place around them; the illegal immigrants were opposing by force their descent from the ships. Again people were injured, again there were stretchers, and again the legendary Mordechai stood out with his courage. The Germans followed in silence from a distance after the hard battle. At the end, everybody was taken off the ships and loaded on the trains. It was noon and the trains began to move.

The descent of the clandestine immigrants in the Hamburg port,
September 1947
(from the collection of French news clips of Shmuel Lutzki,
a mathematician and engineer from Paris)

I'm on a train again, but it's not the same train. This is
not a Russian cargo train whose wheels are ticking beautiful songs along the way; it's a German train—under
British supervision—but German nonetheless. The barred
windows awaken horrific memories in the hearts of some.
Young people were climbing to the windows and beginning to break the bars, while outside along the tracks in
equal distances from one another stood German policemen
and British soldiers. It was crowded, somber and depressing inside the train. The young people bent the bars and
looked outside through them, spitting on the British soldiers
and German officers and yelling "Bevin-Hitler," but it was

nothing more than the release of rage and frustration. The trains moved towards two different destinations—to the distant camp Poppendorf near the northern city of Lübeck they transferred the Ma'apilim from the two ships that violently resisted the descent; the closer destination—camp Am Stau– was where we were heading. The shacks in Am Stau were more comfortable than those in Poppendorf, and it was supposedly a British "reward" for those that descended without a fight. We arrived in the camp in the evening.

The train doors opened and there they were, the wooden shacks, once again, like in camp Ainring. There were many similarities and this had a positive effect on me. I calmed down a bit and told myself that all in all we passed a pretty good time in Ainring and maybe it would be the same here. But there was still a difference. Ainring was an open camp; the movement from and to it was free, but here it was closed by barbed-wire fences and British guards stood at the gates. While I was looking around, we were transferred to the shack, and we ended up in a dormitory similar to the one in Ainring. We began unpacking our belongings when suddenly we were called to step outside. We went out quickly and saw that a food distribution point had been stationed at the entrance to our shack and people were passing by. It was my turn and I received a few pieces of dark bread, the darkest I have ever seen, with butter and honey. Not only had I never seen such delicacies, but they were also so pleasant and tasty after weeks of moldy biscuits on the deportation ships that it was a total delight. Therefore, the memory of Am Stau camp goes through the dark bread, much like the Polish fields go through Kohlrabi, and the Czech city of Náchod through the red and sour apple.

The organization in the new camp was fast and one of its signs was the establishment of a school. I was put in the second grade and we began to study Hebrew and arithmetic once more. In the meantime, it was fall. It was raining, there was a lot of mud on the roads and even the first snow began to fall, to the delight of the kids. The school was often closed for the special occasions we participated in. They were big assemblies, whether for donations to the Jewish National Fund or some holiday. I remember that on one day of snow they took us out to the yard and paired us. A number of kids, including me, were wrapped in signs and fabrics with slogans, while others had the blue box of the Jewish National Fund tied with a cord around their necks. All the kids with boxes would circle around the adults and ask for donations for the sake of the salvation of lands in Israel. This work was done seriously and devotedly. At the end we all gathered in a big hall and important and distinguished people congratulated the collectors, pointed out those that did particularly well and told us about the importance of the Jewish National Fund and the salvation of the land. We kids loved these fundraisers, but the end of the event in the hall was always loud and we weren't interested in the speeches and congratulations.

Second graders on their way to the fundraiser for the Jewish National Fund,
November 1947

The assembly in the hall at the end of the fundraiser, November 1947

Many more events took place in camp Am Stau; there were plays by actors and singers in the hall in the middle of the camp, and there were also circus shows, readings and more. We kids would usually go to the hall with the school and one of the most exciting performances was that of artists from among members of the camp. One such evening I particularly remember was where an athlete and a singer performed.

The athlete had a great body and it was told that there was never a Jewish hero the likes of him since Bar Kokhba (the Jewish leader of what is known as the Bar Kokhba revolt against the Roman Empire in 132 CE, establishing an independent Jewish state of Israel—from Wikipedia). His performance was composed of different routines where he exhibited the strength of his muscles: lifting heavy furniture, weight lifting, breaking bricks with the palm of his hand, etc. But the most impressive part was when he lay on his stomach and a board with protruding nails was laid on his back—the nails pressing against the hero's back—and another participant got on top of the board, jumped on it several times and stepped down. The hero shook himself off, tossed the board away and showed the audience his back to the sounds of great applause. Not one drop of blood was seen on his back and only tiny pink marks were present where the nails touched his skin. A female singer got on the stage after the hero; she sang a few songs in different languages, but mostly Yiddish. One song moved the crowd most of all, it was a song that was dedicated to the bravery of the immigrants of the Exodus and whose tune and lyrics were composed by two people from camp Am Stau. The song opened with the words:

The song is about the Exodus
For its heroes—brave and courageous...

The tune was to a marching beat and this in combination with the lyrics gave everyone a sense of security and optimism and a belief in a better future, in the Land of Israel, of course.

Another event that grabbed much attention was the appearance of a blue closed truck that would circle around the camp. The mysterious truck driver's name was Lustig and he would transmit messages on loudspeakers on behalf of the camp committee, the Haganah and the British command that controlled the camp. Different rumors circulated among us kids about the meaning of the content that was hidden inside the closed case in the truck and about Lustig's identity. As for the case, there were those that thought that it contained secret weapons from the Haganah; others said that British soldiers were hiding inside and through peepholes were checking out the camp (a sort of modern Trojan horse). One kid claimed that it was just a car that delivered milk, but since the case was never actually opened, the mystery continued.

As for Lustig himself, some claimed he was a rat, a spy and a British accomplice, but others claimed that he was a high commander in Haganah who was in charge of the camp and that the supposed British messages that he was transmitting were nothing but encoded messages from the Haganah headquarters in Israel to their people in the camp. Either way, the mystery surrounding the truck was so big that I couldn't resist the temptation and tried to solve it on my own. I followed the truck and when it stopped I climbed a step that was attached to the back door of the vehicle. I peered inside through a crack in the door, but it was all dark and I couldn't see a thing, I tried to make the crack wider and even open the door but I failed. During my attempts the truck began to move with me hanging in the back. The truck accelerated and I was terrified, and only at the last minute, before it left the camp, did I jump from it. I fell and was bruised a bit, but the secret of the truck remained hidden.

Among the messages Lustig broadcast was the repeated promise to us, the clandestine immigrants, that the Haganah would not rest until we all arrived in Israel. The Haganah also promised that we, the people of Exodus, would be given priority in receiving formal immigration papers. Such promises encouraged us and rumors started flying that small groups were fleeing the camp at nightfall and reaching the French coast with fake IDs, and from there making their way to Israel. It turned out that the loudspeaker was a powerful tool, but the British knew that too, so they put a set of loudspeakers on the fences, connecting them to the broadcast center of the British headquarters.

The British messages all focused on attempting to try and convince the Ma'apilim to abandon the vision of immigrating to Israel and reconsider the old plan of settlement in France. For that purpose, a psychological warfare was underway that included news of confrontations between Jews and Arabs in Israel, the dead and wounded in those confrontations, the continued capture of illegal immigration ships, as well as the economic difficulties in Israel. Most of these did not garner any comment, but when the subject of "settlement" in France was brought up, there was growing rage among the people, until their patience wore too thin and they went out to demonstrate. All the camp residents were on the shore circling to and fro in front of the British headquarters, shouting different cries such as "Bevin-Hitler." And then someone threw a plate towards the cables that connected the loudspeakers to the command center, and within seconds hundreds of plates were flying in the air, along with knives, forks, iron bars, bottles, furniture and whatnot. They mainly tried to cut the cables with the plates in order to stop the transmissions, but unfortunately, the shape of the plates made it extremely difficult to achieve a direct hit. This lasted for a long while until one successful shot managed to cut the main cable and silence the transmission. Only then did the atmosphere subside and little by little the people went back to their shacks.

This routine lasted on and off until November 1947. During that month there was a heavy snow, and it was very cold. Occasionally, on class breaks, we kids would go out to the yard and build snowmen or bombard each other with snowballs. The routine continued until a revolution occurred in the day-to-day life in the camp on November 29. During the evening, a big hubbub occurred in the camp, with members of youth movements running around, hugging, singing and shouting: "We have a Jewish state! We have a Jewish state!" It was the day the United Nations decided about the founding of a Jewish state in Israel. The people were drunk with joy; many ran to the main hall and started singing "Hatikvah" and wild "Hora" dancing took over the hall. The celebration, which included enthusiastic speeches and dramatic announcements, lasted a long while. In the midst of the celebration a rumor started that the camps Am Stau and Papendorf were about to close and that we were going to be on our way to Israel again. But among the good news was also news about a great military tension—a large attack by Arab gangs against isolated Jewish settlements.

The excitement was so great that the next day there was no school and the members of the youth movements marched around the camp in their festive garments. In a big field outside the camp, all the youth houses and orphan houses of HaShomer HaTzair gathered and I found myself there as well. A sea of blue shirts, white laces and dark-blue and green ties filled the field, and there were hundreds of kids and teenagers. The instructors organized their cadets to stand in straight rows and each commander had a shape of a square with a missing side (the Hebrew letter *Het*); at the base of each square stood a few instructors and cadets next to two high poles. One of the instructors read out the order of the day to the members of the movement with the summary of what had happened yesterday, and talked about the role of the movement now and about the need to organize for a quick move. There was excitement and tension in the air. When the instructor finished his speech, a trumpet sounded and two flags were raised on the poles: the blue-white flag of the Jewish state to be and a red flag, with the symbol of HaShomer HaTzair. After the flags were raised, the members sang two anthems—the familiar "Hatikvah" and another song that provoked great excitement in me:

We land and sing
In ruins and carcass.
We stride and fling
Through light and darkness.

And knowingly or unaware
We will walk our path.
And with our courageous hearts we dare
To sing and rise again and again.

HaShomer HaTzair anthem in Europe.

Lyrics: Yaakov Cohen, music: popular

Translated from Hebrew: Tanya Rosenblit

It was a sad and quiet singing, but powerful and determined, nonetheless. At the same time we were also saying goodbye to the past, to the camp, to the hateful German soil, to the suffering and the nomadism; on the other hand, there was also the immigration to the long-awaited land, which was about to become an independent Jewish state.

Lag Baomer 1989. *A census of the members of HaShomer HaTzair in Jerusalem—the important tradition continues after all. Thirty-seven years have passed since that census in the forest in Hadera where I had joined HaShomer HaTzair. Forty-two years have passed since the November 29 census in camp Am Stau in Germany. The names of the teams, the style of their speech, and the songs have changed, but the basis remains the same, the tradition lives on.*

Two of my children were standing in the census—one, a senior, was finishing years of activity, the other was officially joining the movement and receiving his blue shirt, like I did in the forest in Hadera. My excitement was obvious

and I told the kids about the song "We Land and Sing" and
about the census of November 29, 1947.

The decision of the United Nations on November 29 had an immediate effect on day-to-day life inside the camp. British supervision grew extremely sparse; the mental strength of the guards had worn out once they understood that the days of the camp were numbered and we would immigrate to Israel, whether they want us to or not. People started leaving the camp and entering almost freely, I even visited camp Papendorf once; it had shabby shacks with round tin roofs.

One day, the long-awaited command arrived, out of the blue, as usual. The command for movement came, and again the famous spectacle of packing our belongings began. We boarded British army trucks and drove south for a few hours until we arrived in a big camp with two- and three-story buildings. It was a German barracks for officers and was extremely comfortable; the houses were white with central heating, a kitchen and comfortable bathrooms. We resided in one of the houses and enjoyed every minute of our stay there. The heat was on at all times and inside the house it was warm and cozy. This camp was also surrounded by a fence but the supervision was very light. Haganah emissaries wandered around the camp freely, speaking to the people and trying to cool down the enthusiasm a bit. They told us that the British were still in control of the land, the beaches and the waters; that clandestine immigrants were still not allowed to enter Israel; and that the British were still the rulers here and that we should be careful not to get too complacent. We were also required to obey a command that seemed very strange: from time to time, the residents of one or two buildings at a time were asked to leave their homes and wander to and fro with no purpose. The adults didn't understand the meaning of that order, not to mention the kids, but everybody followed it meticulously. But when the long-awaited day arrived, I understood its meaning.

After a stay of two weeks in this camp, again—as usual, in the middle of the night—the white sheet was spread in the room, the "visa" camera was flashing again. But this time I wasn't allowed to sit in wrinkled pajamas, so I was dressed in a suit and tie and my hair was combed. "This should be the certificate of a distinguished tourist," I was told, "and not just some poor Ma'apil." With pursed lips I sat in front of the camera, but my heart was happy for I knew the meaning of this. The camera flashed again and again and fake IDs of Polish tourists going for a two-week visit to Israel were prepared at the speed of light. I asked the photographer: "And what if they try to talk to me, how will I answer?" since this worried me, for only my dad could speak Polish. "You either shut up, or answer in Russian—for it is almost Polish," answered the photographer and laughed.

"Passport "photo of a" Polish tourist"

Our belongings were already packed, for what was stuff for vagabonds like us? Who was even thinking about buying merchandise such as furniture, carpets and electrical appliances, and what would we have done with them once the order for movement arrived? No, there was no point in accumulating things and then leaving them behind. For it didn't matter whether we stayed for two weeks, like here, or two months, like in the house with the apple orchard, or even a year, like in Ainring; for eventually, on one unexpected night, we knew we would receive the order and leave with only our backpacks, which was our entire property.

We left quietly in the dark. Three British army trucks were waiting for us, and the truck drivers were dressed in British army uniforms. We got on the vehicles quickly and covered ourselves with canvas so that we would not be seen. The trucks left the camp through a hole in the fence and moved southward. In time, we were told that the operation was organized by Jewish soldiers who were recruited to the British army. They used the equipment, trucks and radios of the military authorities, and thus outwitted the control. Night after night, trucks would leave this way and the camp leaders found a way to disguise the depleting population—to that end the strange order was given to wander around outside without a purpose.

The road kept repeating itself, we were traveling covered by canvas, but we did peep through the slits; we felt the road and guessed the rest. Forests, meadows, destroyed cities, the Rhine River—this is Germany. Again, a checkpoint between the British occupation zone and the French occupation zone, again, the reading of names, cigarettes and drinks for the guards, a few dollars and the gate opened. We traveled towards the German-French border for one last checkpoint and there it was, the good old city of Strasburg. Nothing had changed: the same huge train station, the same hustle, the same women from JOINT and UNRWA, and the same warm reception. Will it all repeat itself? Is it a wheel that spins and returns to the same place? I was afraid it was, that it was all a dream, yet the hope was strong and it overcame all my fears. There was a strong feeling that here I was, saying goodbye to the land of Europe and this time it was final, for good. My will to leave was very strong, yet I somehow felt connected. I remembered the small towns, the houses with the red rooftops, the churches.

I remembered the train tracks, the trains and the rivers. I remembered the church with the piano in the little Polish town, I remembered Náchod in Czechoslovakia.

We continued on our way on other trucks and reached a secluded French farm in the forest that was no different than the old Mizra, but the old French lady with the potato bags was gone. Instead, there were a lot of people from China and Vietnam, as well as others from faraway Asia that came here, God knows how, since there was an ongoing war in the east as well. Many Jews found a common language with the people from the Far East, mainly in the fields of illegal trade, the black market and money exchange. We stayed at the farm for a week; I spent my time wandering around the forests and occasionally saw some Chinese or Vietnamese citizens standing in front of some Jews, bargaining with hand gestures, with delicate bows and courtesy and finally exchanging merchandise and money to everyone's satisfaction.

On this farm, a new "daughter" was added to our family; she was supposed to be part of our family until we arrived in Israel. She was an orphan child, the same age as my sister. She was staying with the other kids from the orphan house for ultraorthodox religious children that had been traveling through Europe since the end of the war. The child lost her parents in the death camps and she was very difficult and unbearable. My parents, my sister and I suffered very much until we finally parted ways. After all, it was our duty to adopt her and help her arrive in Israel and the right thing had been done, despite the difficulties. Thus, all the orphans were scattered around the families, for it was a comfortable way to outsmart the Brits and bring these children to Israel.

Chapter Ten

"And the Mountains Shall Drop Sweet Wine"

That week passed by very quickly and again, in the middle of the night, we got on trucks. By morning we had arrived at the port of Marseille, which was huge compared to the ones I had seen till then. At the port, a French cruise ship was waiting for us; *Providence* was its name. I had never seen such a ship; compared to it the Exodus seemed like a clumsy box. The ship was painted in black and white, and had a big wide deck with many lifeboats and floats. On the deck, close to the stern, was a big residential structure, and under the deck were an infinite number of small round windows that belonged to the dormitories. Sailors and crew members walked around the ship in white uniforms and an occasional black coat, on the sleeves or shoulders of which golden ranks were embroidered.

We boarded the ship and received a clean and spacious berth with white sheets, beds and a small round window facing the sea, all of the highest class—as was appropriate for "respected Polish tourists." In the ship's dining room, everything shone with splendor: crystal chandeliers, china, and candles, and these were set off by dark red tablecloths and napkins. Courteous waiters stood over us, serving food of the most exquisite taste compared to anything I could remember thus far. The captain's look was similar to that of a real captain, like the one in the books: bearded, a white cap with an embroidered golden symbol, white trousers, a short dark-blue jacket with cufflinks and gold buttons. I remembered the captain of the Exodus and thought to myself: how strange was the adult world, for what did the bearded and distinguished captain of the Providence have in common with the wild tramp captain of the Exodus? Which of the two was "the real captain"?

There was not much time to ponder this problem, for there were many diverse and exciting things to do on the ship. A few of us kids gathered—all of us were sons of "tourists" like me—and we ran around the decks, the machine rooms, the navigation room and the club. In the club sat distinguished men playing chess and cards. We had to talk very quietly among ourselves, according to the order that was given by the person in charge of our "tourist" group. Yiddish or Hebrew was strictly forbidden, Russian was partially allowed, as long as we spoke quietly without yelling.

We were forbidden from using the terms "Land of Israel" and "Jews," for there were many Arab passengers on the ship sailing to Egypt and Lebanon—for the ship was to dock there as well. In the tense situation that was already present in Israel, it was best the Arabs didn't know who we were or where we were headed. Despite the restrictions, we couldn't control ourselves indefinitely and a cry in Russian would sometimes burst out. My parents didn't have any time for me or my sister, for they were constantly preoccupied with looking after the "adopted child." She pulled many tricks and would mainly escape and disappear on purpose and my parents would run around the decks in search of her. It was obvious that they needed iron nerves to pass the tests the child put in front of them.

One day, we saw land from a distance. One of the children started shouting "Vitalia! Vitalia!"—"Italy," said an older boy. And indeed, we were entering the strait of Messina that separates Sicily from the Italian boot. On the left side of the strait we saw an indented coast with mountains and small towns along the coastline—all in fog. The right side was much clearer, and the city of Messina could be seen—shining in the sun, with densely built little white houses and a huge port with ships and piers. In the background, behind the city, an amazing image that was new and exciting filled my eyes: above the city stood a huge black and gray mountain with a round and snowy cape with black lines that were breaks in the snow; from the top stood a black and gray pole of smoke that was raised up and buckled eastward. While I was looking at the grand spectacle, the same kid burst out yelling again: "Vezus! Vezuz!" This time no one knew whether the smart boy should be corrected or not. He knew what "Vitalia" was, that is, Italy, he knew (which I didn't know then) what a volcano was and he even knew, despite the disruption, that there is a volcano named Vesuvius in Italy, although the mountain we were looking at was a different volcano called Etna, found in Sicily. Neither the boy nor I had heard about it before, and only years later did I learn what that tall and great mountain was that protruded like a huge smoky lighthouse in front of the Providence on its journey from Marseille to Haifa.

June 1983. *I arrived with my daughter to a small town— Zafferana was its name, and it rested at Etna's feet. The area suffers from heavy heat, moisture and distress. I was searching for transportation that would take us to the top of the volcano, which not only was emitting smoke constantly, but for three months had been emitting lava and ashes as well. Seeing a live and active volcano with flowing lava—which has been my wish for years—almost escaped me. There was no transportation to be found, as the cable car that was supposed to lead us to the top was destroyed by the lava, as were some of the roads; public transportation to the top had not been working for a very long time. After some effort, I found a taxi driver in his house, having* *his siesta. I woke him up; he came out in his underwear and opened the door shouting, but after I offered him a substantial amount of money he agreed to drive us to the top of the mountain, to the station from which guided tours leave towards the site of the lava emissions. The heavy smoke that was curling up from the mouth of the mountain and around the wild, black and ragged terrains of recently formed lava— some of which was still hot and bluish, with smoke and fumes coming out of it—could be seen during our ride up. There was a heavy smell of chloride and sulfur fumes, and our excitement grew. We arrived at the station; a building that once was a hotel was half covered in lava and ashes and looked like one of its walls had stopped the progression of the lava. The smell of chloride and sulfur grew stronger and stung our eyes and noses. The guide led us from there up the mountain, where we got off the vehicle and followed him. We couldn't understand his explanations but they were not needed. We walked along a narrow path, on top of recently formed lava, while on both sides of the path the lava was still hot and soft, and our excitement peaked. On both sides of the path there were cracks in the black outer shell of the lava, and inside the cracks we saw the red hot parts of the lava. Chloride and sulfur fumes came up from the cracks and painted the rocks around the cracks in strong shades of green, white and yellow. We stopped a bit and remained behind our group, and without me noticing, my daughter stepped from the road and said, "Daddy, the land is soft." I grabbed her by the hand and pulled her back to the road.*

"The soft land" was partially melted, unformed lava, and it was dangerous to tread upon. And then the highlight of the tour arrived: we reached a long and wide crack in which red hot lava could be seen flowing slowly. The red, hot, viscous fluid mixed comfortably inside the crack and flowed slowly down the mountain. A stone was thrown into the lava and melted fast, as if it was a lollipop or an ice cube. Our faces were glowing from the heat and the proximity of danger, and strong waves of chloride and sulfur fumes hit our nostrils and eyes again. It was a primeval sight. We went to see more cracks with flowing lava after that. We returned after dark and repeated the route from beginning to end. It was extremely difficult to get enough and leave these sights. The next day, we drove north to the city of Messina in order to sail to the island of Stromboli and see another active volcano. Mount Etna with its thick pole of smoke stood behind us, and in front of us appeared the city of Messina with its white and crowded houses, the piers, the ships and the boats—just like the image I saw so many years ago from the deck of Providence. The strait could be seen as well and like back then, beyond it, was the Italian boot with the misty indented coast strewn with small towns.

The ship continued on its way and entered the open sea; the shores of Italy disappeared beyond the horizon. The mundane and pleasant voyage lasted for several more days and was interrupted only twice: the ship anchored at Alexandria in Egypt and in Beirut in Lebanon. We slowly entered the port of Alexandria, and a few of the Arab passengers were filled with excitement. Some of them wore festive clothes, with some wearing a red turban with a black pompon which had a very distinguished look. The children were also dressed in glamorous clothes, nice suits, ties and hats. The port of Alexandria was an extremely loud and colorful. Seamen, porters, vendors of beverages and sweets, magicians, jugglers and all sorts of other people were shouting and filling the atmosphere. Some got on and off the ship throughout the entire time it remained in the port. I wanted to get off as well, but it was strictly prohibited. Some of the porters wore funny trousers—black and wide with many folds. My father tried to explain to me that these trousers were somehow connected to the Muslim religion that these people believed in, but I couldn't understand the connection.

While the ship was anchored, merchants boarded it, offering diverse merchandise to the passengers. A funny looking individual also came on board. He was bald, wore funny clothes and held a big box made of golden metal with different openings on top of it. The man was a juggler and a magician, and when he stood at the center of the deck a large crowd gathered around him. He had many tricks up his sleeves: card tricks, swallowing fire, releasing pigeons from a hat and rabbits from his pockets, and throwing a large number of balls in the air and skillfully catching them all. But one trick caught my eye most of all, a trick

I was sure had to be one of the wonders of the world: the magician pulled out big metal marbles the size of peaches from the box, took them one by one, put them on top of his bald head and hit them with his fists until they had "disappeared" one after the other into his head and miraculously "reappeared" when they were emitted—again one by one –from his mouth. After several hours all the thrills and excitement of the Alexandria port were over. Some of the Arabs left the ship, others remained and several new ones boarded, and the ship set sail northeast, on its way to Beirut, bypassing Haifa, which was supposed to be its last stop.

Towards noon we approached the beach that looked from a distance like a beautiful and woody ridge of mountains, descending to the sea, with little white houses integrated in the forest scenery. It was so similar to the image of Haifa in July, but still different, a little strange and weird. I didn't have the same feeling I did in Haifa; this was Beirut, a beautiful and mysterious city from afar. I was curious to get off the ship and see it, but like in Alexandria, it was not possible.

July 1983. *The Lebanon war was still raging and its end wasn't in sight. I was sitting with my friends in a beautiful and abandoned villa, which belonged to some Saudi sheikh, in the Druze town of Aley, which was near the city of Beirut. We were the Jip patrol unit, and our job was to* *accompany and safeguard military convoys, tankers and soldiers who were leaving for a vacation in Israel. Our daily patrol started in the east, descending towards Beirut, then continued to the towns of Damour and Sidon and back again. Around us was an inferno of hate; there were ambushes and gunshots from all sorts of armies and organizations against us and one against the other. I counted fifteen militias, armies and armed organizations in this God-forsaken land, and they were all shooting at each other, killing everybody, and we were caught in the middle in the town of Aley. To the west was Beirut, a very beautiful city, and inside it evergreen forests with white houses inside the forest. Sometimes, when the fire subsided, the view became peaceful and picturesque, and then I remembered Beirut of 1947, how I wanted to come to shore and see the city. And here I am, and how I long to run away from this cursed city and never see it again.*

When the shore appeared, some of the Arab passengers got excited again. The ship docked a distance from the port, and boats approached it to take passengers on and off. Some wore turbans like in Alexandria. The atmosphere in both ports was calm, the people—despite their weird outfits—seemed completely normal, as did the children. There was nothing special, except for the prohibition of identifying ourselves as Jews traveling to the Land of Israel, as well as not being able to go ashore. It was very hard to know and sense that somewhere not far away, a few hours' sailing from where we were a deadly war was taking place between my people and the people of these ordinary-looking individuals, with their turbans and suits, boarding and leaving the Providence.

The ship sailed, and Beirut was gone as well. I was overcome by stress and excitement. Were we really going to anchor in Haifa again? Would I see the long-awaited coastline, the woody ridge with the little houses for the second time? Would the ship not turn back again to France? To Germany?! My parents packed their belongings quietly and anxiously. The "adopted" child wouldn't calm down even now, but no one paid attention to her endeavors anymore. It was evening, but we slept in our clothes as everything was packed.

I had a wild sleep again, hallucinating and dreaming. The battle on the Exodus, the old couple crying from a distance without touching the land, the demonstrations in the port, the shining sea, the mist. The dawn was rising on the day of December 31, 1947, an ordinary, chilly winter day. Clouds wandered above the sea, a light breeze blew, there was no fog and the visibility was perfect. I ceremoniously opened the cabin door and stepped outside to look. Only sea!! I ran around the deck in panic and then, at the stern, I saw the sight I was so longing to see: the Carmel descending to the sea. I clearly saw the forest, the houses. It was the coastline; the Land of Israel was in front of me once again, in the palm of my hand, clear and real. I looked towards the port, into the city, and there were cars driving from somewhere to somewhere, train whistles sounded from a distance and at the gate was a crowd of people and children. Their colorful clothes and the blue shirts of the youth movements stood out from afar. The ship approached the pier, the gangplank was prepared and we descended to the rugged pier again. The "Anemones" were still going to and fro, looking and checking, but this time there were no injured, no stretchers, no blood, no constrained rage. The passport check was conducted in an indifferent manner that astounded me. I was still afraid— what if they sensed they were fake, what if we were caught and put once more in the horrible floating cages that were standing there, as if waiting for us. One "Anemone" turned to give me a piercing look, and I was terrified—what if he already knew; could he have sensed it? But nothing happened, the check was over, we passed the port gate into the city, and there we were, inside, the gate closed behind us—as did the circle.

I didn't fall to my feet or kiss the ground; I just stood there hallucinating, dreaming and watching, insatiably swallowing the sights, the white houses, the people and the noisy cars. While I was staring, a crowd of children in blue shirts from the youth movements ran to us, greeted us and shook our hands. A group of boys and girls in colorful clothes were dancing a wild "Hora." In the circle that opened and closed rapidly, I notice the girls in their orange, yellow and brown clothes, singing and dancing:

And the mountains shall drop sweet wine;
And the mountains shall drop sweet wine;
And all the hills shall melt;
And all the hills shall melt.

Amos 9:13, music: David Zehavi

There they were, the mountains, the Carmel Mountains above Haifa, and I sensed the smell of freedom and liberation—a taste I tasted for the very first time in my life. I shook the dream away when my parents pulled me towards the bus that was standing and waiting for us.

That bus seemed like a very strange vehicle; it was long, like a rectangular box, and colored in two shades of green. There were many windows along its long sides. The driver opened the door with a special handle and we started going up the stairs and sitting on paired seats that were organized along the length of the bus and on both sides of a central narrow passage. My sister and I sat on one seat and my parents with the "adopted child" on their lap sat behind us. The singing and dancing continued outside. The bus filled up quickly and many of the families inside it had "adopted children" from the ultraorthodox orphan house. When the bus was full, a bearded man with a black coat

and a black hat boarded the bus, holding a box of chocolates in his hand. Everyone was silent and then the man
asked that all the children from the orphan house raise
their hands. About ten or fifteen children, including my
"sister," raised their hands. The man passed from seat to seat
handing out chocolates to those with raised hands. I felt
as if I had been slapped in the face—after such excitement
and joy, after the warm welcome of the youth movements,
the singing, the dancing, now suddenly this. So what if we
are not ultraorthodox? Didn't we treat the girl fairly? Did
my parents not tend to her needs and suffer because of
her throughout the entire journey? Don't my sister and I
deserve some chocolates? I kept quiet, but my sister started
screaming and loudly demanding her share. My parents
were enraged; then my dad took the chocolate bar out of
the girl's hands by force, despite her screams that filled
the bus. Everyone's eyes were upon us. My dad took the
bar and split it into three even pieces and gave one each to
me, my sister and the girl. The atmosphere slowly cooled
down, the bus started moving and the chocolate issue was
quickly forgotten.

The bus started climbing up the mountain with occasional stops along the way, dropping off some of the
passengers. The ultraorthodox orphan children were long
gone and we remained last on the bus. The bus reached the
top of the hill and kept circling inside the forest and around
the little houses until it reached a small square where it

stopped. Around the square was a road and a sidewalk and in the middle of it there were fenced-in flowerbeds. Two-story buildings stood close to the road and the sidewalk; the ground floor contained different stores. I recognized a vegetable store, with open wooden boxes with cucumbers and tomatoes at the entrance. Another store had writing in blue letters: "Tnuva—Curd, Sour Cream and Cheese," and next to the writing there was a painting of a small bottle. The square was quiet, a horse and a cart wandered around lazily. "This is the Ahuza neighborhood," said the driver. We got off the bus and one of the Haganah members led us to a little hotel. We were put in a nice room with a window that overlooked the forest, the neighborhood and a part of a big valley that lay below us. We were told to stay away from British soldiers and not to chat too much, since our "tourist" visas would expire in two weeks and then we would become "illegal" immigrants, at the mercy of the authorities, once more. But there was no need for these precautions, for the British rule was wavering; most of the "Anemones" stayed in the port area and were almost never seen in Ahuza.

I started going out into the street and walking around, shyly and anxiously at first, but as the days passed my audacity grew stronger and I expanded the range of my walks. At first, I stayed around the Ahuza square looking inside the stores. I liked the "Tnuva" shop; there were strange glasses with a wide base, a narrow neck and an expanding opening with a thick, white liquid inside it. Both the food and the cup are called "labneh" (curd), I was told. I was invited inside and served labneh. The cup was beautiful, but I didn't like the taste inside it. A man took me to the porch and showed me the big valley below us, covered in mist with brown and green stripes. "Those are the valleys," he told me, "Zebulon Valley and Jezreel Valley." He also showed me huge structures inside the valley that resembled yogurt cups (the Israeli Tnuva brand), but they were actually oil refineries.

The range of my walks grew so big that one day I dared to walk on the main road that led from Ahuza to another neighborhood called Carmel Center. The view there reminded me of a pretty big town, much like Náchod in Czechoslovakia; there were many stores and even some noise. I walked to the foot of the mountain and saw the wonderful sight of the Haifa bay once more, the blue sea and the woody Carmel slope—but this time I saw it all from above, from the mountain and up close. There were new details I found from this angle.

Spring 1963. *I was in Haifa again, an instructor at HaShomer HaTzair in the Newe Shaanan neighborhood above the Carmel, living at the same peaceful and quiet neighborhood. The instruction was fascinating, what a wonderful youth. I was walking at the foot of the mountain again watching the big oil refineries. Sixteen years had* *passed, so much had changed, buildings were built, roads were paved, but the refineries remained, the valley remained and so did the Ahuza neighborhood. I visited Ahuza again and saw the same stores and the same houses.*

I traveled a lot with my cadets on the Carmel, in the mountains and forests, and there was no place that was more natural for me than right here to tell them of my experiences on the Exodus. I conducted a series of activities about clandestine immigration, and to conclude we played a game in which all the cadets took part, dividing into three groups: the Brits watching for landing sites of illegal ships, the Palmach—whose job was to smuggle Ma'apilim from the beach into the neighboring villages, and the Ma'apilim themselves. The game started in the morning on the mountain above the neighborhood of Newe Shaanan, and lasted all night with mutual "ambushes" between the Brits and the Palmach down the ridge towards Atlit, and ended at dawn on the beach in an operation of "dropping off immigrants." And so I passed on something to my cadets from my memories of 1947.

The days of leisure and rest on the Carmel were about to end and preparations for another move was underway again. My dad's cousin convinced my parents to move to Tel Aviv—the big Israeli city—as it would be easier to get settled there and find employment.

I was filled with curiosity, I wanted to see Tel Aviv and know what it was like and how it looked. The day of the move arrived. A black cab came to the entrance of the hotel in Ahuza, and we loaded our belongings and drove down the Carmel slope. We reached a particularly bustling place, with buses, trucks, cabs and other vehicles entering and leaving. We walked a small distance and reached the bus that was supposed to take us from Haifa to Tel Aviv. This bus also looked like a long rectangle, but surprisingly all its windows, including the driver's front window, were covered with big iron plates with narrow elongated slots to see through. "What is that?" I asked, "An armored bus," I was told. Half of the road from Haifa to Tel Aviv had to be made in an armored bus, because this road was very dangerous. Arab villages resided on the side of the road and the people there might try to hurt the passengers with stones or even firearms. I was shocked, another war? Indeed? Would it be like on the train running east from Odessa again? But there was little time to ponder. We boarded the bus quickly, and with a groan and a deafening squeak it took off. The road was difficult and bumpy. I tried to peep out through the cracks, but I could barely see a thing. A rain of stones was cast on the bus at some point along the way. "This is an Arab village near Zikhron Yaakov," I was told. The driver accelerated, the rain of stones passed and with it the tension. After a while, the bus stopped, the door opened and everyone got off the bus with a sense of liberation and relief. "This is Hadera," said the driver. "There are no more

Arab villages from now till Tel Aviv and you will continue in a regular bus." We boarded a bus again—this time its windows were open. I was looking through the window and saw a lot of trees with dark-green leaves, there was a tender and pleasant smell in the air, and green, and sometimes orange and yellow, fruits could be seen through the leaves. I remembered the little sweet-smelling orange which we received for May 1st in Stalinabad. They were indeed citrus fruits. We drove through the Sharon country and the citrus kept passing in front of our windows. There were fields too—green fields, village houses, dirt roads. It was a rural view, but it was so different from the Russian Steppe—no sad songs, and no Volga songs; these songs could not be combined with this strange and exotic view.

On the way I noticed concentrations of houses among the trees with names like "Petach Tikvah" and "Ramat Gan." A white city could be seen from afar. Tall buildings could be seen from a distance; where do I remember this sight from? Does it resemble the Czech town of Náchod? Or the French coastal city of Marseille? No, it was not beautiful like Haifa, but still—it mesmerized me in a special way. I lived in this city for the next eleven years. I saw hills of sand, a distant sea, many white houses and little dark shacks too. I was driving in a taxi to my aunt's house, swallowing the city with my eyes, driving along Ben Yehuda Street with its shaded verandas and cafes. The streets were crowded but there was not one "Anemone" in sight. Suddenly, the sense of transience passed and a sense of peace and calmness came over me; it was a feeling that predicted the beginning of my permanent life. No more nomadism, no more new journeys into the unknown. The ship has docked in the home port; the train has stopped with a squeaking sound at the last station. The taxi has stopped. The journey has come to an end.

Epilogue

After several grueling days at the Suez Canal in the Ismailia region, the battalion was ordered to move south, to the city of Suez. Rumors were spreading about another battalion from our brigade that fell into a trap in the city of Suez and there were many dead and injured. We started to move slowly and in the evening we arrived at the outskirts of the city. It was a chilly night in October 1973. I saw a big white city from a distance, which somewhat reminded me of the city of Tel Aviv. War was raging around us, rifle shots, gunshots and smoke; there was fire in the oil tanks in the port. At night, under the cover of darkness, we started moving towards the northern blocks. Nachshon, the commander of the battalion, was conducting the attacks, but he did it with care and wisdom: Shoot first into the windows and doors, then move from house to house, take position, shoot again and move again and so on. In the morning, we came upon a big block of buildings and called it "Katamons." We settled in the buildings and positioned weapons in the

*windows. The front lay ahead with the Egyptians on the
other side of the road. The truce came into effect and was
gradually taking place on the ground. UN observers from
Finland came and established the borderline between us and
the Egyptians. There was quiet, but not for long. Small fire
incidents were slowly developing into an all-out war, a war
of attrition like in the years 1969–1970. We would barely
sleep; at night we would guard the windows against the
Egyptians and during the day work in the barricades and
occasionally shoot towards the Egyptians or take cover from
the whistling bullets.*

*Out there, at the sanatorium among the Sharon
Orchards, my stepdad was dying, the person who has been
my father for the past 28 years, and his last days were in
those orchards that I saw for the first time from the bus
windows, on the way from Hadera to Tel Aviv in January
1948. It was a rainy night, the War of Attrition was ongoing
and it was December 1973 already. I was guarding the post
by the window. Nadav, the platoon commander, entered
informing me in a dry tone that my dad had died, that it
had happened two days ago, but the message was delivered
late because of communication difficulties, and I must leave
at once for the funeral. I didn't say a word. I left the room,
packed a few things and at 4 a.m. boarded the bus that led
me to the airport in Fayid; I was supposed to fly to Israel
from there.*

There was a lot of hustle and bustle, but I couldn't see a thing on the bus or on the flight to Lod. I didn't hear or see a thing—only mists, images, memories and melodies. From the misty Odessa, through Stalinabad, the Volga, Astrakhan, Stalingrad, the Russian Steppe, Smolensk, Szczecin, Náchod, the ruined Europe, Germany, Ainring, Strasburg, France, Exodus, Haifa, France again, Germany again, Haifa again, and finally Tel Aviv. I remembered the hardships and adventures, the moments of grace and moments of anguish. Again, I was asking where my father's grave was, did he even have one? And asking myself about my age, was it fake, were my early accomplishments fake? And if it was all real, then what had happened to me and why? But forging my name and place of birth were necessary, for otherwise I wouldn't be able to leave Russia and who knows what would have happened to me? I may have been executed by Stalin's firing squad and, in any case, how can I even consider life in such a cruel and vicious country?

I was tired. I fell asleep on the flight and awakened at the airport in Lod. I got off the plane and took a taxi, traveling on the road to Tel Aviv again. There were still lemons and oranges along the way, like back then. A sweet fatigue of acceptance befell me. I needed to accept everything I told myself, my distant past, the mysteries of the life and death of my first dad, the fact that I had two fathers, the bag of memories and the road that was so difficult for me because of the distant past. I saw the white city at a distance again;

tall buildings, white houses, and an echo came up from the sea from afar. Old songs were playing in my head, in my ears, in every part of my body: "Volga, Volga, oh Mother dear...", "We land and sing...", "And the mountains shall drop sweet wine and all the hills shall melt...", "Misty, misty mists..."

APPENDICES

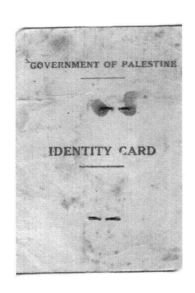

January 1948 - My mother's fake ID card from the British Mandate

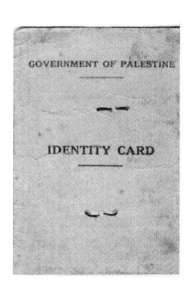

January 1948 - My father's fake ID card from the British Mandate

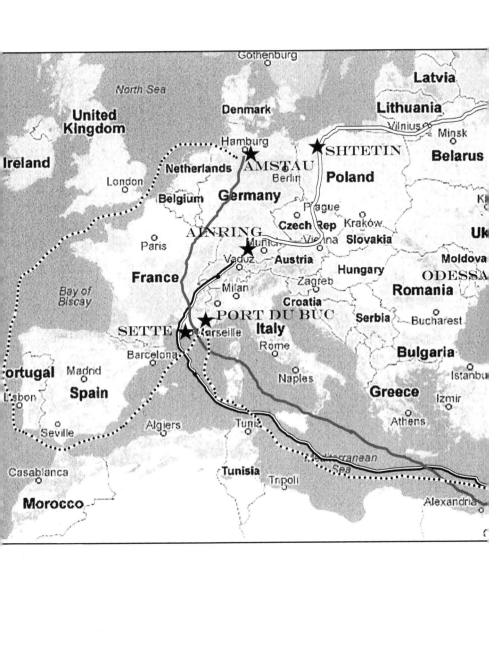

Made in the USA
Columbia, SC
24 August 2018